For Mothers, By Mothers

54 Empowering and Diverse Stories
About Motherhood from Around the World

created by
TISHA LIN

For Mothers, By Mothers
Copyright @ 2018 by Tisha Lin

For information, please send email to info@tishalin.com.
First trade paperback edition 2018

For information about special orders, or to inquire about author speaking engagements and events, please send email to info@tishalin.com.

Published by:
Empower Every Mom LLC
www.formothersbymothers.com

Tag and Follow: @tishatlin
                  #formothersbymothersbook

Manufactured in the United States of America

Cover Illustration by Deb Heyrana
www.heyrana.com

Cover Design and Layout by Carla Green
www.claritydesignworks.com

Photos of Tisha Lin by Katherine Pimentel Photo
www.katherinepimentelphoto.com

Editor: Amanda Colin

ISBN: 978-0-692-17938-3
Also available in ebook and audio book formats.

To all mothers — of the past, present, and future...

Let us pass on the timeless wisdom of mothers
from one generation to another...

To:

From:

Contents

Why This Book Was Born.................................. ix

The Motherhood Manifesto xii

– Stories –

Chapter 1
New Mother Transitions

Hiring the CHO (Chief Household Officer) – *Majken Linnea Zylik*..5

Fairy-Mama Friends – *Kinda Yaghi*...........................7

A Tale of Two Breasts – *Mia Verdoorn* 9

Staying True to Yourself – *Shile Ismaila* 11

Worries and Wonder – *Vanessa Caqueiro*.....................13

Chapter 2
Empowering Births

All is Well – *Carolina Alvarado* 17

Birthing the Mother Within – *Paloma Devi*....................19

I am Woman – *Alicia Ling Horsley*...........................21

Free to Choose – *Sandra Herrera*............................23

Chapter 3
Mother-Child Connection

Balls and Dolls – *Emy Alonso* 27

Unraveling the Mysteries – *Carrie Dienhart*. 29

Hearing Wisdom in the Silence – *Kate Brenton*. 31

Mothering is a Rite of Passage – *Mira Groff* 33

Chapter 4
Sacrifice and Fulfillment

Choosing Both Worlds – *Chhavi Mittal* 37

Building Blocks of Love – *Mariela Albrizio* 39

Beyond the Mommy Role – *Youmna Tayara* 41

Chapter 5
Compassion

When "Bad" Works for You – *Luz Leal* 45

A Child's Gift – *Corinne Morahan* 47

Lessons in Spilled Sauce – *Jimena Mosquera* 49

Chapter 6
Inner Guidance

The Power of Mama's Intuition – *Jessica Martinez*. 53

Trusting Your Mothering Instincts – *Amy Witmyer* 55

Double the Love – *Sara Bernard* 57

Chapter 7
Parenting with Purpose

From Clothes to Compassion – *Abigail DeCerbo* 61

The Gift of Presence – *Janine Tandy* 63

Sacred Duty – *Jordanna Nativ* 65

Little E for President! – *Theresa Pang Law* 68

Full Disclosure – *Lynn Kane*................................71

Chapter 8
Healing and Transformation

Spiritual Encounters – *Eida Wong*...........................75

Learning to Love Myself – *Amanda Colin* 77

Finally Free to be Me – *Tracy Lin*............................79

Coming Home to the Heart – *Catalina Cabrera* 81

Mother, Heal Thyself – *Ibetliza Frias*.........................83

Leadership in Motherhood – *Lisa Guillot*.....................85

A Single Mom's Spirit – *Nadia Estrella* 87

Mama Phoenix Rises – *Toni Leone*...........................89

Progressing, Step by Baby-Step – *Yolanda Peruffo*...............91

Chapter 9
Strength

The Sunshine after the Storm – *Zaida Zamorano* 95

Stronger than Yesterday – *Lisandra Gutierrez* 97

Birth Power – *Jackie Montoya*...............................99

Surviving and Thriving in Motherhood – *Phillipa Yoong*........101

Mumma on the Move – *Ariel Blyth* 103

Gifts from the Moon – *Querube Elena Alvarado* 105

Chapter 10
Trust and Surrender

Making Peace with One – *Karina Alvarez Bogantes* 109

The Mysteries and Power of Pregnancy – *Katie Silcock*. 111

Reborn with Passion and Purpose – *Tisha Lin*. 113

Chapter 11
Lessons in Parenting

The Mama Juggle – *Maria Jose Leal*. 119

Peeling Back the Bubble Wrap – *Carla Green* 121

Learning as We Go – *Melissa Berger* 123

Chapter 12
Blessings and Reflections

Adventures in Motherhood – *Mina Poler*. .127

Born of the Heart – *Laura Dolloff* 129

When Spirit and Earth Collaborate – *Gloria Pérez-Molina* 131

Breakfast for Dinner – *April Haberman* 133

A Letter to My Dear Darling Boy – *Eve Thong*. 135

45 and Fabulous – *Jennifer Iky Kinslow* 137

Write Your Own Story. 140

A 10-Minute Restorative Meditation Exercise for Mothers 143

Acknowledgements and Gratitude. 145

Contributors Index. 147

About the Creator of this Book 149

For Mothers

By Mothers

Why This Book Was Born

This book was created very much like growing a baby. I had been wanting to create a book for mothers for some time. But the moment never felt right, until it was. The idea for this collection of stories came to me like a bolt of divine lightning. I saw it in its fully manifested physical form, and from that moment I knew it would be born into the world.

As if being pregnant with its energy, it gestated within me. It grew and developed over time in the creative space of supportive mothers who all helped along the way. From its website, to its beautiful original cover artwork, editing, and the carefully thought out design elements — a true labor of love. Together, we gave birth to this very special, unique offering of support and love to the world. The spirit and soul of this book hope to inspire and reclaim connection, compassion, and the ancient oral tradition of storytelling amongst mothers.

In "village culture", mothers always mothered together, because motherhood was not, and is not meant to occur isolated and alone — but rather in a close, supportive community.

However, in our modern, busy, overworked times, mothers are finding themselves frustrated, confused, and overwhelmed. And while we have email, texts, and chat groups to connect on some level, mothers are still struggling with depression and anxiety over all the changes and responsibilities they are managing.

Much of the wisdom shared by mothers has lost its in-person storytelling format and tradition. There is so much nobody tells you when you become a mother. You're just figuring it out by trial and error as you go along.

Fortunately, there is now a growing revival of women's circles and support groups and we can all benefit by marrying some of the old and the new approaches and perspectives on motherhood. However, *it still takes a village to raise a child.*

The Intention and Ripple Effect of this Book

Women become mothers through many different routes. Some by surprise, some with intention, and some by force and violation of their bodies. Yet, once we have our children in our arms, we look upon them with love and want the very best for them.

Motherhood goes beyond borders, cultures, and language. There is an understanding, empathy, and connection that only mothers share with one another. Regardless of race, status, nationality, personal beliefs, and even sexual orientation, on the field of motherhood, there is equality.

All loving mothers share the same cares and worries. We celebrate the milestones that our children reach, and we feel joy in their magical and spontaneous moments. We delight in their smiles, giggles, hugs, and kisses. A part of us wants them to stay young and cuddly forever. Another part of us cheers them on as they grow up, become adults, and find their place in the world.

As mothers, we all experience times of frustration and impatience. And yet, the daily practice is finding our way back to love and connection with ourselves, and also with our children. We are all works-in-progress, learning with each day on this extraordinary, life-transforming path of motherhood.

This book consists of 54 empowering stories from mothers around the world — single moms, divorced moms, step moms, adoptive moms, expat moms, stay-at-home moms, career moms, mompreneurs, millennial moms, grandmothers, combinations of the previously stated moms, and many more emerging roles of motherhood.

The following stories illustrate the range of inner resources that mothers possess, such as courage, resilience, wisdom, and love. These collective voices are also putting an end to shame, guilt, isolation, and separation.

This book is a tribute to every loving mother — of past, present and future.

It serves as a sacred text to be passed onto our children, our grandchildren, and to all the special mothers in our lives. By sharing this book, we also keep the storytelling tradition alive for the generations to come.

Whether you chose this book for yourself, or you received it as a gift, I am honored that you are reading these very words and I hope you will feel inspired and empowered by the stories in this collection.

The intention of this book is also to help and impact the lives of children and mothers beyond its readers. Therefore, net proceeds of the sales of this book will be donated to nonprofit organizations that support, educate and empower the lives of mothers and families.

To stay informed about these contributions, events, and special mama gifts, please sign up to receive our love notes at www.formothersbymothers.com

No mother should ever feel alone in her struggle. Together, we can create a powerful ripple effect of support and love for mothers all around the world.

This is the book that every mother should have. Gift a copy to all the special mothers in your life!

With Love and Gratitude,
Tisha

The Motherhood Manifesto

As mothers, we are often re-mothering ourselves.

We are healing deep wounds.

We are breaking unconscious cycles of violence and abuse.

We are coming to learn of our own true power.

We are reclaiming our voice and speaking our truth.

We are forgiving — both ourselves and others.

We are freeing ourselves from suffering.

We are owning our human imperfections,
our wisdom, and divine intuition.

We are stepping into unconditional love every single day.

We are raising tomorrow's leaders, innovators,
peacemakers, and trailblazers.

We are changing the world and creating
a ripple effect of profound love.

By Tisha Lin

~ *Stories* ~

"Tell me a fact and I'll learn.
Tell me a truth and I'll believe.
But tell me a story and
it will live in my heart forever."

— *Native American proverb*

Chapter 1

New Mother Transitions

"When mothers feel seen,
heard and understood,
everybody wins."

– Tisha Lin

Hiring the CHO
(Chief Household Officer)

ONLY FOUR AND A HALF MONTHS after giving birth to my firstborn flawless baby girl, I faced the reality of going back to my full-time career in digital advertising. So much had changed for me, yet I was more afraid to be at home and deal with the unknowns of taking care of a baby than to go back to a stressful corporate job, simply because it was predictable. Well, at least more predictable than a baby!

At the time, I was ashamed of this feeling and my lack of confidence to take care of the beautiful baby girl that I had just brought into this crazy world. I wasn't a natural mother, I would always say, so of course, I would go back to work. Then began the search for the perfect nanny. Now, if this isn't one of the scariest things to do as a parent, hand your child off to a stranger, then I don't know what is.

We met with several people referred from our local mom's network and we stumbled upon a very special woman. Unlike other parents who researched nannies in great detail, we actually decided on this woman because it felt right. From the moment she walked in the door, she was focused on my daughter. She swept her up and spoke softly in a language I could barely understand. But I knew from the tone that there was a deep tenderness in her words.

My friends thought I was nuts for hiring someone I could barely communicate with since she only spoke Spanish. My husband could communicate with her though and somehow I made the language barrier work. We found our rhythm and our collective language and soon she became the CHO (Chief Household Officer). And as I began to trust her more and more, she quickly moved into the role of a third grandparent.

Sound like a dream come true? Now here is where the trouble begins. As this woman cared with every ounce of her soul for my daughter, my little girl became attached — very attached! She was heartbroken the minute our nanny tried to leave. And as you can imagine, watching my child scream as I take her from this woman's arms was also heartbreaking for me.

I asked, "Is this *really* happening? How can my child love this woman more than her own mother?" Yet every day, as she grew older, the bond between them remained as solid as ever. This woman loved my child as one of her own. My gift of an amazing nanny had now become my source of pain.

Every day I would wonder if my child would ever love me as she did her caregiver. I sat in meetings distracted by the thought of what they were doing throughout the day. It consumed me.

And now eight years later as I write this story, I look back on how naive I was to think this way. This child, my firstborn, has an endless amount of love for everyone in her life, including her first caregiver (now retired but still in our lives).

As for our bond, it is unbreakable! The ironic thing is, when I share this story with her, she gives me a silly look, laughs and says "No way, Mom!"

Majken Linnea Zylik
Mother of two beautiful children

Fairy-Mama Friends

EVERYBODY EXPECTED ME to get back to my normal activities a week after my baby was born. Friends and family wanted to come over and see my newborn as soon as I had delivered (even at the hospital). The issue was, I was having difficulties breastfeeding and needed to pump every three hours. This was not a task that I felt like doing in front of everyone else.

I was also so exhausted. I wasn't up to getting advice from random family members about why my baby was not latching properly, or hearing a list of other possible reasons as to why breastfeeding wasn't working for me.

I feel like in my Arab culture people do not really value the time and space a new mama needs when she gives birth, and it can all become very overwhelming. I didn't want anybody around.

Then some of my mama friends started to come over. They would offer real help with the baby, like feeding my newborn or putting him to sleep while I was pumping. I started to realize that I didn't have to filter my words around these other mothers, I didn't need to try to impress them. It was such a relief. They understood exactly what I was going through, and what I needed the most. I finally started to feel comfortable having other people around to help.

Now that those early moments have passed, I have come to realize that honest motherly advice is the best! There are tons of books and articles available, and they are wonderful, but your mama friends are the ones who can truly get you through the challenges of motherhood.

In addition, contrary to what you might be thinking, you should not feel guilty about asking for help or admitting that you don't know what to do. Ever. Every new mama needs a fairy-mama friend who can help her adapt to all the ups and downs of motherhood and remind her to take care of herself.

Let's face it, when you're a mom you haven't got time for drama and gossip in your life, so choose your friends wisely. You want a friend who is supportive, loving, and understanding of the limited amount of time you have to socialize.

As mothers, we need friends who understand what we're going through, friends to whom we can rant to about feeling like a "bad mom" without being judged. And, when we are at our lowest, we definitely need a friend who can remind us of how great a mother we are. A true mom friend understands that you crave adult time and will do anything to make plans with you. They will then be okay with you canceling your plans at the very last minute because your kid is not in the best mood, or because you're simply too tired.

Along the journey of motherhood, you're going to hear a lot of judgment and a lot of advice. People are likely to pressure you, often out of love, and you're going to feel overwhelmed, but at the end of the day, only you know what's good or bad for your child. Always follow your instincts, and find yourself some mama friends to back you up!

Kinda Yaghi
Mother of Samy

www.theshareddiaries.com

A Tale of Two Breasts

MY BREASTFEEDING JOURNEY started like many first-time mothers — eagerly. I couldn't wait to put my baby to my breast as soon as she was born. I felt super ready for it all. Little did I know that I would end up having an unexpected C-section. Due to this, I was only able to start breastfeeding her an hour after she was born.

The problems started with her unbelievably strong suck. That little thing was thirsty! This resulted in cracked nipples and the rest went downhill from there. No matter how hard you try to keep your breasts and nipples clean, bacteria will always find a way of entering the cracks and that's a way for mastitis (an infection in the breast tissue) to form. Pair that with your first milk coming in with force and you've got a recipe for complete disaster. Angry boobs!

One breast was twice the size of the other, completely red, and inflamed... It looked furious with me. Every time the baby latched on I wanted to faint in pain. I was in tears at every feeding. Even though only one breast was affected by mastitis, both were excruciatingly painful and sensitive when breastfeeding.

My doctor immediately put me on antibiotics for two weeks, assuring me that it wouldn't affect the baby's milk. Stopping breastfeeding and pumping wasn't an option for me because stopping suddenly would have only made it worse and could have caused an abscess. So I resorted to pumping the affected side, and only fed her directly on the unaffected breast. After two weeks, it still wasn't better and I had to continue on the antibiotics for two more weeks.

In my perspective, antibiotics can do a lot of harm. Antibiotics kill ALL bacteria–both good and bad bacteria. This increases the likelihood of yeast overgrowth and that causes Thrush, a condition in which candida (a yeast-shaped fungus) overgrows. "Good" bacteria is needed to fight off thrush, and since you don't have any good bacteria (thanks to the antibiotics), it's like the perfect storm. Yeast feeds on sugar, and breast milk is nice and sweet. Most women generally tend to get thrush in the vaginal area, but it decided to take up residence in my breasts, along with the mastitis.

After one month of antibiotics, I had to take a month's supply of thrush medication for the yeast infection. All of this while still breastfeeding and pumping. Pumping somewhat helped, because it wasn't as painful as the baby's latch, but I can't say it was pain-free though. Even the slightest touch or accidental bump would cause me to wince with pain. I was taking very strong ibuprofen twice daily, just to be able to make it through the day.

Honestly, the pain never really went away. Perhaps I just got more used to it. Besides the physical pain, there was quite a lot of emotional pain as well. Here was this beautiful newborn baby girl whom I absolutely love and cherish, but every time she cried I shuddered because I knew I needed to breastfeed her, and I knew I'd have to endure that pain. It really took its toll...

I managed to breastfeed for six months and froze enough breast milk for her to have one bottle a day for another month. I wish I could have breastfed more, and I do feel a certain amount of mom-guilt for not keeping it up longer. But being depressed, in pain, and constantly on the verge of tears wasn't doing my baby any good either.

Some critics might say I was selfish in my decision, but at the end of the day, it was *my* decision and I stick with it.

Mia Verdoorn
Mother of Freya Gwen

www.theshareddiaries.com

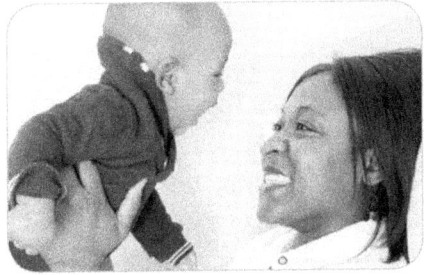

Staying True to Yourself

WHEN I BECAME A MOM, I was far away from my family and didn't have much support around me other than my husband. I struggled with various issues that many new mothers face.

When my son was born, he didn't latch onto my breast properly and the nurses told me that we might need to get him some therapy. But for the first four weeks of his life, I just kept trying with him, and thankfully, we eventually made it and I was able to breastfeed him.

Little by little, I learned to understand my baby's "language". I started to understand when he was hungry and when he wanted comfort and to be held, all the differences between his various needs. It was a process and step by step, I got help and tried to go with my gut instincts. With time, I became clear on what I was and wasn't comfortable with.

My own mother had five kids, and therefore, her own ideas about raising children. The times that she came to visit, it was actually very difficult. She had her own point of view about what I should be doing with my baby. But it was really important to me that I could do what I felt was right for me and my baby.

When my son turned two years old, I decided to go back to work and was lucky to have an amazing nanny for four years. However, due to unforeseen circumstances, my nanny had to eventually leave and finding another with the right requirements has not been easy ever since for me.

I've actually had about six different nannies since my son was born. For me, it's been about finding the right person that I can trust with my child, and who can respect the rules and guidelines of our home. If any candidate I meet is not comfortable with this, then I continue to look for someone else who can work with and my family's values.

This is an important theme for me as a mother — to embrace my own definition of motherhood, and to not let anyone compromise the way I want to raise my child. I strive to raise my son as a happy, healthy child who knows how to love and respect himself. Along this journey, I too am learning with each day how to be happy with myself, who I am, and what I have achieved as a mother and a woman.

As a result of my motherhood experiences during these past seven years with my son, I was inspired to create an online community for women of African origin to come together, encourage one another, and explore their own unique experiences of motherhood.

Hearing from other mothers has always given me great comfort, not that I necessarily need to do things in the same way, but just to have other mothers understand, empathize, and offer support means the world to me.

Shile Ismaila
Mother of Kamil

www.africanmommy.com

Worries and Wonder

ONCE YOU BECOME A MOTHER, things are never quite the same. But this isn't necessarily a bad thing because you get to watch how the simplest things bring so much joy, and how small things can make such an impact on your child.

For me, watching how my child can be so fascinated by a small action, like pressing the button on the TV remote control which leads to turning the TV on is amazing. It is simply wonderful to see my child smiling because of the lamp hanging from the ceiling or his excitement when watching the washing machine go round and round.

Motherhood changes you. Putting your child first becomes the most normal thing to do. You can't always eat when you want, or take a shower...or even go to the bathroom! And finally, when you can, you most likely won't be alone!

Most of the conversations you will have will be about your child, and things you normally wouldn't talk about become super normal like farts, burps, poop, and pee. It's almost like all the "normal" adult conversations were left behind when your child was born. And another thing, it's also not uncommon to miss your child who has been asleep for just an hour in the room next to you!

Worrying is also a big part of motherhood for me. In the beginning, I worried about my baby's weight, about the number of wet diapers he had, about his feeding, and sleeping. I even worried about just being a mother.

As my baby grows older, some of my worries go away but new ones appear. As his motor skill development evolves, there are more things to worry about and things to be aware of. For example, the repeated "area scanning" starts as I look out for possible dangers such as electrical outlets, small pieces he can put in his mouth, sharp edges that he can bump his head on, places where he can clamp his small fingers, and so many more. The good thing about being worried is that it keeps you alert and helps prevent many accidents and unwanted incidents.

Motherhood is simply amazing and we can learn so many things from our little ones. Just by looking around us, we can start appreciating all the small things in life.

And when things are difficult, just look at your child who loves you more than anything and thinks you're the most amazing mamain the world.

Vanessa Caqueiro
Mother of Lorenzo

www.norwegianmuminportugal.
blogspot.pt

Chapter 2

Empowering Births

"Whether born of the womb or
born of the heart, but still, born into
a life of unconditional love."

— *Tisha Lin*

All is Well

I HAD TWO VERY DIFFERENT birth experiences — first with my son and 15 years later, my daughter, Maia.

I gave birth to my son naturally at a very young age. So when I became pregnant again, although many years had passed since my first pregnancy, I was sure I was prepared to have another natural birth with my daughter.

While pregnant, I was able to keep up my swimming for almost nine months. I practiced prenatal yoga and walked often for exercise. I didn't experience any symptoms or discomfort during the first trimester. It was a great pregnancy!

Until one day at 39 weeks pregnant, I went in for a routine check-up with my gynecologist. I was starting to feel contractions but based on my first experience, these were early labor contractions and I could've continued on fine.

However, when the doctor checked my baby's heartbeat, the palpitations started to slow down and I felt really scared about this. I was then admitted to the hospital and was told that it was highly probable that I would end up having a C-section.

I got really upset and started to cry. My doctor told me that the longer we waited, the more risk my baby would face. I felt very nervous in the hospital and I told myself that I would not end up having the surgery. Nonetheless, that's exactly what happened. Ultimately, I wanted my baby to be safe. So I was prepped for surgery and in I went.

Once the operation was over, I was brought back to the hospital room where I waited for them to bring my newborn baby girl to me.

The moment I saw my daughter, all the nervousness that I had felt about the surgery faded and I realized that all was well. When I held her in my arms for the first time to breastfeed her, I felt an instant bond and connection full of love.

Now, reflecting on the experience, I can say that I don't regret having the C-section. It went very well and I never felt the pain that I've heard other moms talk about. I recovered quickly.

But most importantly, my daughter was safe and healthy! We both were.

I don't believe that this experience made me less of a woman or mother. In the end, I think it's the well-being of both mother and baby that is essential — however the birth occurs.

My daughter Maia is now four years old and regardless of how she was born, naturally or by cesarean, she is healthy and thriving in her life! And we are so fortunate that from the time she was just one month old, she has slept through the whole night allowing all of us to rest well also.

Carolina Alvarado
Mother of two wonderful children

Birthing the Mother Within

I SPENT MOST OF MY LIFE dreading the thought of becoming a mother. I had immense fear and anxiety around the subject and often caught myself thinking that "my life would end" if it ever happened to me.

Then, it happened. I found a great love (now my husband) and for the first time considered doing the crazy thing that I thought I'd never do. I had a beautiful pregnancy and could feel I was growing a very strong and very large baby.

Forty weeks passed and I found myself beginning my labor. I had scheduled a home birth with a wonderful team, midwife and assistant, doula and my beloved. That was it. Although I had my plan, I was prepared for anything to happen.

Four days of labor and I still had not dilated sufficiently. My team assured me that my baby was healthy and all was well, but because my baby was large for my size, my body needed more time to accommodate for his size. I was desperate and exhausted. At that moment, my doula made me a Yogi Tea and the quote on the bag said, "Nature does not hurry, but all is accomplished." It was then that I understood all was well. I just needed to relax and trust my body to do the perfect thing. I could forget the concerned voices of family members and the internal pressure I felt. I affirmed that if another four days of labor were necessary, I would embrace it.

No rational person looks at an acorn and scorns it for not already being an oak tree. I felt that this irrational pressure was something I was probably working on in my own life, and I would be wise to allow the beauty of natural unfolding. That I could trust my son's soul to bring him in at the perfect moment. Active labor and dilation followed my realizations and 20 hours later, my 9 lbs 1 oz baby boy was born strong like a little bull.

Through this process, I feel that a part of me did "die" when I became a mother and it's now when I am actually starting to live!

The birth process is one where we both are born again. Allow it to be an experience of learning and self-reflection. Get ready for any expectation to be shattered as you climb the rungs of your existence. Have faith in your body and heart's abilities to stretch and break open in ways your mind will never understand.

We have the spiritual support of the generations of grandmothers before us and are bound to the community of mothers that unites us in this unspeakable love.

Paloma Devi
Mother of one divine son

Sacred Chant artist + Creator of the Vocal Moksha Method
www.palomadevi.com

I am Woman

"I'm sure my body will know what to do," I recall saying blithely. I was six months pregnant with my first child. We were seeing a private gynaecologist I had only been able to afford with my parents' help. Nothing is too much for our first grandchild, they insisted. My firstborn paid the price for my arrogant folly, being born prematurely by seven weeks, enduring a cascade of interventions that ended in forceps, pneumonia and three weeks in NICU. He was four days old before I was allowed to touch him.

After three horrific hospital births in the space of four years, my mothering soul was crushed. I had nightmares and long spells of dark, angry months. Thanks to the internet, I found other mothers, equally abused. "Birth rape" became a bitter part of my vocabulary. However, attending my sisters' hospital and home births steered me towards healing.

In December 2016, I realised I was pregnant again after ten years. My husband encouraged me to have counseling and this time, he threw himself full force into helping me have a home birth. I doubt I have the words to do justice to the wonder of the experience. The pregnancy was peaceful and I learned to rest without guilt. Flying a midwife over for the birth was a large expense, something I would have normally shunned. However, I viewed the cost as an investment in my emotional and mental health, as well as in the best outcome for my baby.

I was in prodromal labour for two days and filled the time with good conversation, nice meals, and taking extra care of my family. Real labour did not begin until over an hour after my water broke. I was filled with excitement; I was going to meet my baby!

When the contractions began to hurt, adrenaline coursed through my veins. I became a warrior focused on bringing forth life through my body. The outside world faded and the precious privacy of being at home allowed me to reach into the deepest parts of my soul; where I am Woman, elemental and infinite.

I love all of my children, but I now realise that the love I had for the first three was rooted in desperation and fear; a belief that more harm would somehow find them. This birth transformed my love for them. It is still ferocious but also hopeful. I am no longer a fearful dog backed into a corner with few choices available to her, but a majestic bear that can protect, provide, and inspire.

Good births bring forth strong, connected mothers. The value of a whole mother to a child is incalculable. They are mothers who can and will fulfill the needs of their children. And a person raised in love, whether or not there is material wealth, will make this world of ours a brighter and better place.

To all the mothers before me, I salute you. To the mothers by my side, I am here for you, and to the mothers yet to be, recognise the privilege and miracle you will perform and do right by yourself and your child.

Alicia Ling Horsley
Mother of Bern, Katelin,
Cian and Evan

Free to Choose

FROM THE TIME MY PREGNANCY BEGAN, I would ask myself, "Will I be strong enough to handle the pains of a natural birth?" And each time, the answer I heard from within me was "No." And that's why, despite the disguised judgments from people close to me, I decided to have a cesarean section.

I thought that this decision would make me less strong somehow. I thought that I would be a weak mother. However, none of that mattered when I held my baby girl in my arms for the first time. She was born on June 25, 2014, at 7:12 p.m. There she was — the best part of me, with her little eyes slightly open.

I still remember when I saw her from the other side of the operating room. She was looking for me the same way she looks for me now, three years later, with that same impatient love. And then, in that moment that felt like time was standing still, I closed my eyes for a while longer as they finished up the surgery.

Today I can say that having the surgery was the bravest act for me, as a woman — to face that separation from my baby, and at the same time, transmit all my love to her with such determination.

That's why I impress upon every mother to do everything with that same pure love. Because even in the face of the most difficult situations, if that unconditional love is present, then the weight of it all will be lighter and passing.

Sandra Herrera
Mother of Sofía

Chapter 3

Mother-Child Connection

"We are here for the imperfect and
magical journey of motherhood,
not the illusion of perfection."

– *Tisha Lin*

Balls and Dolls

SOME TIME AGO, when I was just a young girl, one of my best friends jokingly asked me, "And if you have girls, will you give them to me then?" Because I had always wanted to have boys and that's exactly what happened.

When I was a little girl, I always played with balls, not dolls. And for me, as I saw it, it would have been a bit difficult to start out on the road of motherhood with "dolls".

When I was pregnant with my first baby, people would ask me if I wanted the baby to be a boy or a girl. I always told them that first and foremost, I wanted my baby to be healthy, but that I would love it if the baby was a boy. Regardless of whether I was having a boy or a girl, I knew I would enjoy motherhood so much and that is exactly how it has been from the beginning.

Something else a lot of people used to say to me was, "I hope it's a girl so she can take care of you in your old age." I have always felt that motherhood is an experience beyond giving and giving of oneself. It's about sharing achievements and accomplishments too. I don't see motherhood as an insurance that guarantees a "daughter-nurse"to be with me as I grow old.

Ironically enough, I was recently taken in for an urgent surgery, my oldest son was the only one home in the city at the time. His special way of handling the situation made me feel the love, support, and care that so many had said I would get if I would have had a girl when I was pregnant.

To that, I say: It's not necessary to have a girl, a daughter; just know that in the times that matter the most, your children will show you in their own unique way all the dedication you have given them without expecting absolutely anything in return.

Although I am a mother of two sons, I have had the opportunity to realize the importance of a healthy mother-daughter relationship as well. When I finally decided to make peace with the decisions my mother had made with me and to love and appreciate her for who she is, it changed the way in which I relate to her.

As a result, that decision and shift within me had a surprising effect on my relationship with my own sons. It created a relationship that became more and more filled with harmony, mutual support, and love. Without a doubt, each of my teenage sons has their own uniqueness and this makes living all together very special.

For me, being a mother is the most amazing role in my life and I live each day full of gratitude for this incredible opportunity. Thank you to my two companions for life!

Emy Alonso
Mother of two wonderful sons

Unraveling the Mysteries

MANY OF US HAVE AN EXPECTATION that your love for your child will be a perfect love; that you will bond immediately — forever. That may be true for some, but not all.

Our children aren't always who we thought they'd be, or, dare I say, who we hoped they would be. Some fortunate people have a child that is just like them, a little twin, and they have a special lifelong bond. And some of us have children that couldn't be more different from us, and more so, some children are much more difficult than others. This is where the real parenting task comes in.

It's easy to love an easy child. It's another thing altogether to wake up each morning and show love and patience to a child that makes you want to pull your hair out. You may not like your child at each stage of growing up. And if you're having trouble bonding, at any stage or age, know that your relationship will continue to evolve, grow, and change over time.

My first baby never smiled at me. He refused to hold my hand. He wouldn't let me hold him or comfort him. I felt like I was a bad mom. I felt like he didn't like me. He has had a number of diagnoses that have required experts to navigate. As I write this, he is ten years old and he continues to be a mystery in some ways. He definitely continues to be a distant child, and I still sometimes wonder if I'm a bad mom, or if he even likes me.

But, every once in a while, he brings me a little thoughtful gift to show me he loves me, and it is incredibly moving every time he does.

This is definitely not the picture I expected when I became a parent. My second son is also giving me quite a challenge. No "typical" child here. But, every day reveals a little more. Every day I see them and love them for who they are.

No matter who your child is, every day is another opportunity to connect and to show them love.

Carrie Dienhart
Mother of Louis and Mark

Hearing Wisdom in the Silence

ONE LATE NIGHT, I held my newborn son — he was about three weeks old. As he cried and cried, I shushed, swayed, bounced, and tried to nurse, but nothing, nothing, nothing worked. Sleep deprived, recovering from a long labor and an unexpected C-section, much of my lifelong certainty and strength was unavailable to me.

I wondered what I was doing wrong. Would I ever get this Mom thing right? Would I ever sleep again? What did I have to do to make him stop? And mid-sentence, I stopped.

I realized that all the advice and not-so-subtle questions I had received from others (many relatives) about pacifiers, schedules, night routines, and books and articles with three, five or seven steps, were all targeting the goal of silencing the child. Shush, baby shush.

In that moment, with his little body in my hands and his cries ricocheting against the night and against my heart, I softened. Rather than shush him, I listened. I asked him what he needed. What did he want me to know? I explained to him that I was listening and wanted to learn what he needed. I said I was sorry that I missed the obvious for so long.

I told him that he was the most miraculous being I had ever known. And I promised him that no matter what happened in life, he would always find me in his heart. I told him that I would work to be the best mother that I could be and that some days, I would completely bomb. But I promised that I would always work to get better.

I told him everything that night. I can still feel that moment — this little being was a whole person intact. He was his own universe, and he had just arrived and was trying to figure it all out. He didn't need to be silenced. He needed to know that someone was listening to him.

I realized that most of the parenting language out there these days is about the parent, and not about the child. I realized all of this in that second, the way life does, in moments which are larger than ourselves. Moments when it's so clear that we have to work to maintain the wisdom they bring to us. We hear our breath differently; everything slows, and everything makes sense — including ourselves. We, my son and I, had that moment. And he stopped crying, for a bit. And that bit, that is the golden grace of parenting.

The experience changed me as a mother. But, let's be honest. We went on to many other sleepless nights, fumbles, and chaotic moments (even now, he is teething). I spend a great deal of time shushing, swaying, singing "Baby Beluga" and nursing to assuage the crying.

But that one night remains as our foundation. That one night I understood that it really is just the two of us. While our family has more than two, the mother-child bond is something altogether different. Honor it. Cherish it. Protect it. Nurture it.

Motherhood takes it all and gives you moments in return that help everything else make sense. The most important thing you can do is listen to yourself so that in the middle of the night you can hear the whisper of grace that is your child.

Kate Brenton
Mother of Aaron

www.wisdomofone.com

Mothering Is a Rite of Passage

As SOON AS MY PRECIOUS DAUGHTER arrived in my arms, her newborn tears ceased and mine began. And at that moment, our indescribable connection was born unto its unique journey.

I am a mother that strives to be present, comforting, fun, loving, honest, inspiring, dependable and devoted. As a parent, I have experienced many moments of profound love and connection, as well as times when the physical demands are enormous, the emotional needs seem insurmountable, and the vastness that once felt like boundless bliss took on a cloudier hue.

When my daughter was around four years old, it became apparent to me that I was going to have to expand my scope of understanding and deepen my reserves for presence and patience. I found myself being challenged by the emotional demands and vast expressions of her personality.

This delicate, yet fiery little girl was doing her best to assume control of everything. Her verbal outbursts, lack of cooperation, and endless tears weighed heavily on my heart. I wanted to support my daughter's expressions and opinions, yet much of our time was spent in negotiations. The joy and connection that we were so often in celebration of was becoming more difficult to access.

This was a troublesome time for me, as I didn't feel prepared for the challenges that were arising. I finally found a quiet moment and realized that my daughter's seeming desire to be in control was really a call for help.

It seemed that her inner world felt unreliable to her and she was grasping for a sense of security. Although I was showering her with tremendous love, I felt at a loss for how to offer her what she truly needed to be able to express her fears in a way that would bring release and relief. I wanted to remove this pain for her so that she could spread her beautiful wings and enjoy the many facets of life experiences.

But I knew that I could only help guide her "to the well", and that she needed to "drink the water" herself. At this point, I opened up to my community to receive some support and wisdom.

In walked the *Hand in Hand* parenting tools, and truly, a new reservoir was birthed in my heart. Through these powerful techniques, my daughter and I created a powerful pathway to deepen our capacity to heal, open, release, and transform.

As I cultivated the capacity to set healthy limits and remain present and loving through the emotions that resulted from them, my daughter was able to settle into a security that allowed her fears to diminish and her self-assuredness to grow. The more she released her fears, her insecurities lessened, and her confidence and inner safety expanded. I began to see such profound changes that I started to explore more of the *Hand in Hand* approach. Through patience, believing, listening, playing, and holding a safe, timeless space for transformation, we have established a trust and communication that has fostered a sense of inner security, courage, and freedom.

At times the effort seems large, but the inner rewards for both of us are far greater. We continue to thrive in our relationship based on conscious connection as we honor the Light in one another. Her tears are my tears, her joys are my joys, my patience is her blessing, my openness is her celebration, and my limits are ultimately her freedom.

Mira Groff
Mother of Tulsi

Chapter 4

Sacrifice and Fulfillment

"If you're a stay-at-home mom,
never say that you don't work."

— *Tisha Lin*

Choosing Both Worlds

BEFORE I HAD MY BABY, I had a completely full work schedule and absolutely loved it. I had imagined that once my baby was out of my tummy, I would be ready to get back to work. However, I could not have been more wrong.

I had absolutely no clue what I was in for because nothing anyone tells you can get you ready for motherhood more than the actual baby in your arms. This was surely true for me, especially because I had sailed through my pregnancy with glowing skin and an active routine.

The second I had my little one in my arms, I realized that this little person needed me so much! I was never going to be able to leave her at home and go to work. Being in a nuclear family dynamic, I had to depend on domestic help a lot and I hated it. So I took each day as it came. I fought to rise above postpartum depression and channeled my motherly "superpowers".

But before I knew it, it had been two years since I had worked and this was a great source of unhappiness within me. I hated that I had to choose between two things that I loved — my work and my baby.

I finally got back to my acting work and made my comeback in a television show on one of the leading networks. But now I was going through a struggle of an entirely different level. How could I leave my daughter at home for 15 hours straight every day? I left when she was asleep, and I came back only to find her sleeping again. Oh, that guilt! And how I missed seeing her smiling face.

I again found myself at a crossroads. "No," I told myself. I thought about it hard. I continued to work on that show for only a month and then decided to quit my lucrative career as an actor and start something of my own in order to balance my life and live the best of both worlds.

I chose not to choose. I realized that my life is with my child, and if something is not connected to her, then it's not right for me. The second I realized this, the guilt flew out the window and in came the motivation! My husband was supportive enough to join me in my endeavor and this was the best decision of my life. I worked from home for two years before I took up an office space directly opposite my house where I can easily walk to.

I am the proud co-founder of one of the most successful and loved Digital Content Platforms of my country. Now, I not only act, but write and edit, and I have learned a variety of other roles to play in content creation. All the while, I also get to spend my mornings, afternoons, and evenings with my child. It's the best of both worlds for us.

So, I believe that if I can be a mother, which I see as the world's toughest job, then there is nothing else I can't do.

Chhavi Mittal
Mother of Areeza

www.chhavimittalofficial.com

Building Blocks of Love

IT'S NOT EASY TO RAISE THREE KIDS so close to each other in age — especially when they are all two years apart! I never wanted a nanny at home to take care of them, so I put my professional career on hold and dedicated myself to my kids. I only had the help of my mom.

I would take them to school, to their recitals, and to school meetings. I helped them with their homework. I took them to the doctor, to ballet, to swim class, and to painting classes. Maybe that sounds exhausting. It was. But time goes by so fast, and soon they were all grown up and independent.

Today, I am grateful for the three marvelous children that I have. They are mature, professional, sensible, service-oriented, and empathetic to others. They are happy and that is what is most important to me. After all that is said and done, it was the best decision I could've made at the time. To weigh my professional life with my role as a mother, and that I even had the luxury to do so. And if I had to do it again, I wouldn't doubt it for a second. I would choose to be with my children all over again.

They have been my life teachers. Each one is different. Each one has nourished me as a mother and as a person. And with each day, I continue to learn from them. We have cultivated a wonderful relationship and now that the three of them are adults, I realize that I did a good job. And it shows in how they live their lives and how they face their challenges.

Now I await the gifts and blessings from them — my grandchildren! That's when love multiplies, where one loves without anguish and responsibilities, and when we give of ourselves completely. It's a second time around to enjoy the miracle of life.

As a mother of three grown children, my advice to new mothers would be to step into their role from a place of love and patience. Because motherhood should not be a burden, but rather an experience that you enjoy every second because the time flies by. You blink your eyes and your children have flown from the nest.

So consider fewer restrictions and more authenticity. Remember to hug, kiss, and caress them more. These are the building blocks that create healthy human beings — physically, emotionally, and spiritually. From the moment you decide to bring your children into this world, they are your priority.

For me, from the moment I found out that I was first pregnant, being a mother has been the most enriching experience of my life.

Mariela Albrizio
Mother of Jose Alejandro,
Oriana, and Valentina

Beyond the Mommy Role

UNTIL RECENTLY, MY KIDS DIDN'T REALIZE that I had done anything with my life before I became their *Mommy*. They thought it was "so cool" when they found out that I was a former TV news anchor. My seven-year-old was super impressed and asked if I could please go back to what I was doing, but also still be their mommy.

This question is at the heart of a struggle that so many mothers face. It's about the sacrifice some of us make when we become a mother and potentially put our careers on hold to raise our children.

I am an expat mom, so in addition to leaving behind a career that I had worked for and succeeded at for many years, this sacrifice was about following my husband on his own career path which took us to Angola. As many expat moms will tell you, leaving your job and moving to a new country can be exciting! However, after a few months, it hits you right in the face: this exciting, new country is now normal, and the way that you are living your life is no longer fulfilling.

Being away from home meant that I didn't have my closest family and friends around me. This brought up additional adjustments to deal with, on top of getting used to being a mother (which is a 24/7 job).

Motherhood is a venture that keeps your head thinking and worrying every second of every day. You wonder whether you are doing the right thing with every small decision or issue. Then, when you feel the need to take a tiny little break, you look around and notice that you don't have the privilege of having your loved ones with you while you live abroad. You don't have a support group to turn to or lean on when you need some quiet time.

As a mother, wanting a break is not telling your kids you've had enough of them, it's simply refueling for a couple of hours (not much). This time off is so important in order to be able to then give your kids your full, undivided attention when they need you.

There are many transitional aspects of motherhood. You become a new person and you're constantly figuring out who this new woman is along the way, but especially during the early years of life together.

Finally, my kids started school and I suddenly found myself with a lot of free time on my hands. Once again, I wondered if I could do something meaningful with my time on top of being a mother.

My children and I are growing together. They are still young and I try to give them everything they need by being their *Mommy,* but I also acknowledge that in order to give to them, I also need to give to myself. I need an outlet to do what my heart longs for.

As a result, I started a new chapter in my life and have happily been able to return to one of my passions: working with the Kambamba School Project team. This initiative supports hundreds of underprivileged children and helps them to receive an education.

So in answer to my baby's question, "Yes, I can definitely go back to work and still be your mommy!"

Youmna Tayara
Mother of Karim and Judy

www.expatmommyangola.
blogspot.com

Chapter 5

Compassion

"Mothers make history every single day.
Their lives may not be televised or public,
but they are no less important."

– Tisha Lin

When "Bad" Works for You

"YOU'LL UNDERSTAND WHAT REALLY BEING A MOM means when you become a mom." That's what my mother used to say to me, and I'm sure that at some point, many other moms tell their children this as well.

Now that I am a mom to my only son, Juan Diego, who is going through his so-called "terrible twos", I understand completely what my mom meant! But to judge is easier than to understand and I have to confess that I have judged. Sometimes I still judge, but I am learning how not to.

We, as mothers, don't all do things the same way, nor do we make the same decisions. We haven't all had the same lessons come through, and at times, that may make us judge each other without even realizing it.

Today, after almost three years have passed, I still remember an experience that blows my mind. When Juan Diego was just two months old, we went out for our first family outing. It probably lasted no more than a half hour. We went out because staying at home all day was driving me crazy. So to clear my head a little and change the scenery, my husband suggested that we go for a walk at the mall.

While out that day, I got a lot of looks and whispers. I heard one woman say, "Poor baby. He's so small, he must be cold." And while she didn't say it, I swear that I almost heard her say that I was a bad mother. At that moment, I almost burst out crying, but held it in and didn't say anything. My hormones seemed like they were going crazy during that time and I did not want to ruin our first outing together as a family.

I think that if that experience were to happen to me today, I would have the courage to tell that mother that my baby feels very comfortable, wrapped up in his stroller, and out with his parents. And I know this because he didn't even wake up that day.

The truth is, I felt happy because it was our first time out in almost three months. I had brushed my hair, put on makeup and a nice dress for the first outing with my husband and my baby. It was then that I also realized just how easy is to judge others, perhaps without even knowing it, and without understanding what a first-time mother is going through during this new chapter of her life.

I have had many more experiences similar to this one. But what is important is that with each day, my role as a mother helps me to judge less, and to be more empathetic and compassionate toward others. I can now better understand that when a mom isn't running after her kid all the time, maybe it's because she is just tired of running. If a mom lets her kid get dirty and run around the restaurant screaming, maybe it's because she is hungry and wants to actually eat. If a mom arrives late to work, maybe it's because her kid didn't want to go to school that morning. And if a mom asks for help, it's probably because she really needs it.

So my conclusion is, doing things that other moms might consider "bad" or "wrong" isn't bad at all if it works for you and makes your family happy. It's actually really good.

Luz Leal
Mother of Juan Diego

A Child's Gift

UNLIKE MANY LITTLE GIRLS, I did not dream of becoming a mother. In fact, when my husband and I got married, we discussed openly that we most probably would not have kids. However, after we were married for a few years, we both felt called to become parents. We were both "good" kids who got along with our parents, and we just knew that our child would be the same.

The birth of our son was miraculous. It was drug-free, calm, and serene. Yet, life with him was anything but. The first few months of his life, he seemed plagued by unhappiness and an awareness far beyond his years. At just six weeks old, friends declared that they thought he was a genius. His precociousness was not simply mesmerizing, but it was at times, odd.

Motherhood for me, for many years, brought very little joy. I had many, many moments in the early years of asking myself why was it that I was his mother, feeling like another, more compassionate mother would have been better for him. I constantly felt like I was letting him down. I could never provide the stimulation that he needed. I didn't know what was "wrong" with him, or me for that matter.

Six years later, we discovered that in fact, he was and is an exceptionally gifted child with a superior IQ. While this sounds like something to be proud of, gifted children have special needs. They often feel frustrated and isolated. They are different from their peers and experience high levels of anxiety and depression at a young age. There is little support for parents of gifted children because unlike other kids with special needs, giftedness and intelligence are highly valued in our society. But few people see the struggle for these children and their families behind closed doors.

Once we had a diagnosis, we had a roadmap of where to look for answers and were able to find a school for him where he would be with his peers. However, I spent years prior to my son's testing beating myself up. Thinking that if only I were stricter, less strict, more loving, less indulgent, less structured, more playful — whatever it was that I felt I was not, that he would be "better". I have now come to realize that the organization, structure, and most importantly, love, that I have parented my son with have helped him turn into the lovely, joyful, loving boy he is today.

Those rough years in the beginning have made these past two years, and the future ahead, that much sweeter. Yet still, I wish I had known that you can never know who your child is until you meet him or her. I wish I had known that I was being the best mother to my son that I could have been. I was giving him exactly what he needed, even though it didn't feel like it at the time. I wish I had known that seeking out professionals and getting answers is not a weakness, and can lead to an amazing transformation. I wish I had known that there were others in the same boat as I and that things would get better. Ultimately, I wish I had known that my son was perfect — that there was absolutely nothing "wrong" with him.

I'm so thankful that it only took us six years to uncover our son's giftedness, because he has a lifetime ahead of him to get the support, stimulation, and love he deserves. And I now have a happy, healthy, and amazing little boy to love.

Corinne Morahan
Mother of two wonderful children

www.gridandglam.com

Lessons in Spilled Sauce

SITTING ON THE KITCHEN FLOOR that morning was probably one of the hardest "mama moments" I've ever had. Teriyaki sauce was splattered all over the floor, and the fridge was oozing with a bittersweetness from the day before.

That day before still reverberates, bringing up raw and real memories to remind me that deep down I feel that, in this day and age, it's not safe to live in a woman's body. I had experienced a "Shakti awakening"— whatever that means, as I still don't truly know. It had felt like "ecstatic orgasms" as I lay on my shaman/doula/massage therapist's table.

It was a remembrance of what I had always known was possible for all mothers, for all women, and it heralded the beginning of a reclamation. But, at that moment, I had no words to express the immensity of what had happened and continues to transpire.

And so, on that next morning, after what felt like the worst hangover ever, I found myself pleading to God, to the heavens, to anyone listening to come back and show me the way. But no one came. There on my kitchen floor, I felt utterly alone...

What had just happened? My tired "mama body" of six, four, and two-year-olds was on the floor, sitting, as I bawled my eyes out. I had screamed at my daughter, and not the first time. And, now, I had shamed her, my first-born daughter, for dropping the teriyaki bottle and splattering its entire contents everywhere.

Again, my daughter had made a mistake. Her imperfections, her way of turning my head upside-down, her way of being "too much" reminded me and pressed at my sore spots. She shone a light on all my own imperfections, on all the ways that I was not perfect, and on all the ways in which being human and messy and imperfect were not okay.

Memories spanned an eternal sorrow, and I wished for that eternal embrace that never came. I wept while I windshield-wiped the floor clean, again and again, like a scene from "The Karate Kid" movie. It was as if I needed to clean away my own shame — my shame at the pain of being so utterly human.

That moment and teriyaki sauce now hold a sweet spot for me, as reminders that, yes, oh yes, I am wholly and utterly human, and that it is my divine practice here on this earth to remember and embrace all of it — and of how Grace does come to rush in. "She" wants to come in disguised, in different sauces, spilling and seeping in through new sacred stories, while I continue to embrace my imperfections, our imperfections.

To my children, thank you for continuing to spill and seep in through all of the cracks, inviting me to drink all of life in.

Jimena Mosquera
Mother of three perfectly
imperfect lil' big humans

Chapter 6

Inner Guidance

"A mother's intuition is like any muscle.
It just needs some toning and
practice to grow in its power."

– *Tisha Lin*

The Power of Mama's Intuition

I SPENT MONTHS ON BED-REST that would've been far too much for many others. But for me, there was always something inside of me that just knew — I was sure that she would come, even though at the beginning things were so uncertain.

I clearly remember the day that my obstetrician mentioned the possibility of not continuing with the pregnancy because it was risky for me. This set off the alarms of worry for my husband and many others who were following our story from a distance. With each day, the worries and questioning of our family and friends grew. But I repeat — something in me always knew.

In between the bleeding, bed rest and the constant doubt of my loved ones, the certainty that I'm referring to continued to declare its presence. One day, it was a dream. In another moment, it was a movement or rather, a response from my little one within. That inner voice that seemed like a soothing call that did not stop ringing. I also faced each day with my husband's supportive care and love. And as each day went by, more confidence grew. I knew not to doubt. She was coming.

I didn't have a baby shower. Nor did I have time to set up a room or go shopping to pick out her clothes. But I felt really happy to be able to share each moment with her — my baby swimming inside of me. It was one of the times in my life that I have felt the most present to the moment itself.

And finally came the day of my birth. It came early, of course. Everyone was terrified. My husband didn't stop crying. My mother looked at me as if it was the last time she would ever see me. There were extra doctors present and my own doctor was warning everyone that this birth could be a miracle!

Seeing all of this was as if I was watching a movie on the big screen. Yet, there I was. My hands just felt my little one inside, wanting to come into this world. And just three hours later, my baby girl Anais would see light and feel the cold of that room. Her cry would subside when they put her on me, skin to skin. I can still remember her size, just right for the eight months of life that she had spent inside of me. My little baby girl yawned a little smile as she heard my voice call her by her name and welcome her to the world.

Today, after almost eight years have passed, as a mother, there has never been another moment of my life when I was more connected to my own human nature. Each experience of motherhood is different, just like each phase is unique. But what prevails still, is the confidence and communication with the inner guidance that awakens within us when we become mothers.

Nobody experiences motherhood in exactly the same way. That's why it's of utmost importance to gain that trust in knowing and understanding that our intuition is directly connected to the umbilical cord that connects us to the life of that little one growing inside.

Never doubt your intuition when it is communicating with you. It always knows.

I dedicate this story to my own beloved mother, Isabel. May she rest in peace and know that our souls are eternally connected.

Jessica Martinez
Mother of Anais

www.jessicamartinez.yoga

Trusting Your Mothering Instincts

FROM MY EARLIEST MEMORIES, I always knew I wanted to be a mother and to birth my baby my own way! It was a deep and primal call. Sharing my story here has allowed me to reflect on my experiences of being a mama to my one and only son for the past 18 years.

Birthing my baby was the most powerful and transformational experience of my life! But, still, the early period was not easy. There was a lot of loss. There were twists and turns, and, at the age of 28, I moved from marriage to divorce, and became a single mom. To navigate this tough leg of my journey, I had to dive deep and trust my mothering instincts even more. I defied many odds to protect, reclaim, and grow both my own and my son's lives. Despite obstacles, disapproval, and lack of support, I trusted and listened to my instincts, and honored my wild heart.

A few years later, when I was 31, I met the love of my life! After five years of wild magic and deep healing, we got married and became our family of three. For myself, I don't feel that I, alone, would have been able to bring in the other influences and teachings that my husband has brought for our son. For my husband's contribution, I am forever grateful.

Now, together, my husband and I continue to raise our son, who has truly become an outstanding, wise young man. We have always parented our son with free and open communication on every subject, from the mystical to the mundane, and from sexuality to spirituality. We can look back and celebrate the miracles, the magic, and the deep transformations arising out of all our wild journeys together. They have been both bitter and sweet!

Now, at my 45 years of life, my most powerful message to all mamas is—trust your mothering instincts! Every woman and mother needs to find her own unique path, her own voice, and her own style. There is no one way or right way, or even an easy way.

For myself, I had to learn how to really trust and embrace my mothering instincts and wisdom. I had to learn how to listen very deeply to the messages from within. I learned how to honor my own wild heart, and what that truly means to me, on my terms. This helped me become crystal clear on my mothering intentions. Then, I became able to help my own son to find his own unique path, voice, and style.

Now, even as I write this, our family of three is starting a new chapter together, and we are ready! Our son is graduating from high school and preparing to spread his wings and fly off to college.

Everyone can access the truth of their own wild heart through the practices of deeply listening to their own innate instincts and wisdom. Trust and listen….

And so, to all the grandmothers, mothers, and mamas-to-be, I offer my deepest bow of gratitude to you. I place this offering of love at your wise feet, from my wild heart to yours.

Amy Witmyer
Mother of Juaquin

www.amywitmyer.com

Double the Love

I AM A MOTHER OF TWINS, a girl and a boy. When I got pregnant people constantly told me all of the things I was *not* going to be able to do with them, like breastfeeding, carrying them at the same time, caring for them with no extra help, travel, or just having a life!

For me, some things did feel impossible, but they were fewer than what most people expected. When my twin babies were born, I wasable to achieve some of my goals — specifically breastfeeding and taking care of them, just the two of us, my husband and I. However, carrying them both at the same time was one of the "impossible" things. Maybe I started too late, maybe when I saw Ezra complaining I didn't try hard enough, or maybe I just needed an extra pair of hands to try more. But honestly, when I did have that extra pair of hands, I preferred having help to carry one of the twins while I carried the other. Whatever it was, it doesn't seem to matter much now. I'll try again if I ever have another set of twins!

I am not a supermom, nor do I have superpowers. But I managed. I think a mother of twins struggles as much as any other mom, not more. I think I managed because I am resourceful. When something would go wrong, I focused on how to make it right. I didn't pity myself when other mothers weren't having the same issues as I was.

Since I became a mother, I've looked to other moms for support and friendship — this helps to not sink at the first sign of a storm and certainly gets one through the challenges of motherhood with a smile.

I know that I'll see the results of my choices and actions with my kids later in their lives. Meanwhile, I'm watching them as they grow and evolve and I know that I am not doing that "bad".

Even now, people still tell me it's going to be difficult. They never say it's going to be fun. And yet, my twin babies are almost eight months old, and the way they look at each other, smile at each other, or look for one another just melts my heart.

Don't ever let negative comments get to you because ultimately, nobody knows what you are capable of.

Sara Bernard
Mother of Twins Nara and Ezra

www.pequenospasajeros.com

Chapter 7

Parenting with Purpose

"May our children be free and imperfect.
May our children discover their own joy.
May our children grow up with magic in their hearts."

– Tisha Lin

From Clothes to Compassion

FOR ME, PARENTING HAS AND ALWAYS WILL BE the most exhausting, challenging, sometimes gut-wrenching, and soul-searching journey I have ever taken; a journey I wouldn't trade in for the world because it has also been the most fulfilling, inspiring, and deliriously joyful privilege I have been given.

To think that I have been bestowed the opportunity to raise these two amazing, beautiful little girls (who are not so little anymore) fills me with both fear and contentment. Will the decisions I make about what they eat, what clothes they wear, what sport or instrument they play affect their futures? But at the same time, how absolutely incredible is it to see my daughters grow into their own and make these decisions for themselves.

We are bombarded every day with the dos and don'ts of parenting that we begin to second guess ourselves at every turn. Now that I have had 14 years of parenting under my belt, the one principle my husband and I continue to practice is balance.

Sure, it's important for them to eat their veggies and protein, but it also doesn't hurt to have a huge ice cream sundae or a slice of cake every once in a while. Yes, we monitor their screen time, but when it's been a long day, and we all need a break, it certainly is ok to watch another video or play another game on their cellphone.

As a mother of two girls, I relinquished my "rights" to choose their clothes a long time ago, but we still definitely try to steer them towards "tasteful" clothing. However, what if one of them wants to wear some crazy fishnets (deep breaths mothers of daughters, it will happen) under holey jeans? Well, so long as the holes are not excessive and body parts are not hanging out, why not? After all, she did pair the outfit with some awesome Docs. Or if one wants to wear the same ratty t-shirt out again, so long as it's clean, we let it go, and then perhaps suggest shopping so we can buy a new one.

They know when it's time to get serious and buckle down with their homework and school activities. They also know that not everything is about getting good grades and going to an Ivy League school.

It's also about the human connections they make and the people they inspire along the way. So in all that we do, we really try to maintain this balance. As my girls grow and start to express themselves and figure out who they are and what their place is in this world, we need to be able to show them that it is okay to let loose, make mistakes, figure things out, and not know what they are supposed to do next.

This is all part of navigating our world so that they can become productive, responsible, and compassionate citizens. And, if they can see that my husband and I try to live our lives with balance, the two of them will emulate us and do the same as they reach out and make their mark.

Abigail DeCerbo
Mother of Izabella and Sabrina

The Gift of Presence

ONE OF THE MOST IMPORTANT MESSAGES and heartfelt sentiments about being a mother that I can express is the importance of showing up. I have found that being physically and emotionally present for my daughter is everything.

We have quite a deep foundation of love and a strong bond that solidified early on. I wanted to be there for all of her "firsts" as much as possible — her first steps, explorations, cries, needs, and questions.

It is important for me to allow her to emote and express all of her emotions, not just happiness, but sadness, fear, and frustration as well. It's also important to me to be able to explore these emotions with her, so she feels safe in communicating her thoughts and feelings. To know that this is being authentic and that it's perfect as is.

I am lucky that my work of teaching yoga allows me the gift of time with her, and that it's not just the amount of time, but the quality of our time. When we are together, I do my best to not have the distractions of social media, phones, and other things that we unknowingly allow to eat up our time. This is so my daughter can see that I am listening, interacting, and there for her.

Of course, it's not always like this 100 percent of the day, as emails need to be answered and there's work to be done. But we really do have such amazing conversations and time together doing art and casually chatting about life and her day. This experience is the gift of presence that we give to each other. Our relationship is really nourished by all that comes out of the simple moments and activities of everyday life.

As a mother, it's also important for me to talk to my daughter about how I am. So if I am feeling sad, angry, content or anything else, she understands that everyone can feel a range of emotions at different times and that this is healthy and normal.

Each morning, I always make sure that I wake her up for school by saying "I love you to the moon and back." I end each day with these same words.

To me, everything about being a mother is exemplified by fully loving and taking in all that my daughter is.

Janine Tandy
Mother of Penelope

www.nourishyourself.biz

Sacred Duty

AFTER AN ALL TOO COMMON MELTDOWN in my closet while attempting to get ready for an event, I had this lightbulb moment that changed the course of my life.

Tears in my eyes, puffy red face, I reflected on the episode and realized I called myself every horrible name, doubted my own beauty, and insulted every article of clothing in my closet. I realized that if I continued to behave this way, speak this way and live this way, then my daughter, then only a few months old, would grow up to do the same.

Not anymore. I needed to figure this out for myself and then help others do the same.

Our little ones learn from our example first. They learn about eating habits, self-talk, personal care, confidence, how to dress, speak and behave alone and in public, and ultimately how to be a human in this world. They will wonder about the necessities of food when you skip meals but insist they eat.

Self-loathing comments will be repeated during dress up after watching you get dressed in stress each morning. Mindless snacking will be mimicked while watching a movie after countless evenings seeing you zone out on the couch.

As they grow, they'll source relationships that feed and breed negativity when your confidence lacks. They'll grow up and give up on their goals and themselves in vicious cycles after seeing you do the same.

We have a big job and most of us go about it unconsciously. No one tells you about the immense responsibility of being a mama. No one tells you about the *real job* beyond food, clothing, shelter, and snuggles.

It's impossible to highlight the endless life lessons that can be instilled into our little ones in a light-hearted conversation with a newly pregnant friend. It's a journey that's discovered by each of us as we go and grow.

So after many years on this journey, here is some of the motherly wisdom I have gained through experience. We, mamas, have all the answers inside of us, but we aren't always sure how to access those answers. For most of us, our intuition isn't developed enough or loud enough to be heard right away. We aren't always confident enough to listen to its advice and power, so we rely on the Internet and online groups for parental advice.

I'll confirm, it's okay to have personal interests and have a family at the same time. That the best of us are in fact whole women with robust interests, lives beyond our children, and feel a sense of accomplishment in sharing that journey with others.

In a society where families are spread apart, women play many roles and the demands on our time are endless. We need to share our secrets to continuously raise one another up.

Generations continue to destroy themselves from within while all the answers were waiting in our hearts and minds all along. We just need to find our strength, conviction, and one another to make our messages heard. It's our duty to set a better example for the next generation that we are collectively raising while healing our own wounds.

There's empowerment in parenting. I want each mother to feel it so she can teach it.

Everything you want for your children, you should also want for yourself. Everything you teach your children, you have an opportunity to learn for yourself. Every life lesson is there for you and your entire family. If you didn't learn it young, you have a second chance!

This kind of power doesn't exist anywhere else in the world. This power is held by every mama. Many are simply unaware. The power to influence a generation is at our fingertips and speaks to us every day through our intuition. Every thought, action, reaction, and movement forward rubs off on our little ones. The better we are, the more we heal our wounds. The healthier our choices and the stronger we love ourselves and the people around us, the more they will too. The power is in positivity and listening to our intuition.

At some point, every day, remind yourself of this inherent power you so beautifully hold. Cherish it and bring it forward at every mommy moment because that is your power in action. Set the example, live the example, and create humans that spread that example.

If you're a new mama, I know it seems scary. But from one mama to another, I have confidence in you.

Jordanna Nativ
Mother of Scarlett

www.inspirediaries.com

Little E for President!

WHEN I BECAME A MOTHER, I promised myself that I would never compare my kids to other kids — that my children would be the best part of my husband and I and that would be good enough for us.

But on one fateful day, when the U.S. presidential candidates were still on the road, Little E, my son, came home and said that a classmate at school had told him to "Go back to China. Trump is going to kick you out!" So Little E asked me if he was going to be sent back to China because he was *not good enough* to live in the USA. I was furious that someone could say that to him — he was only six years old. He didn't understand or deserve this. He was born on American soil to an American citizen. How dare someone tell my son that he was *not good enough* to stay.

This really triggered the part of me that never felt "good enough" growing up as a child. There were three daughters in my family and the token only son. I was in the middle and it was never easy to keep my own identity. I had to find my sense of self outside of my family. My grandfather and father always protected me and made me feel special. They always noticed me. My grandfather would always tell me to stick up for myself especially when people looked down upon me; indifferent to the fact that it could be my own family. Both my grandfather and father loved and protected me, and made me feel that I was good enough, just as I was.

And so years later when my own son came to me, feeling sad and hurt with his tear-stained face, I kept myself calm and told him that he was in fact *good enough* to stay on American soil because he was a good person. I told him that he has never hurt anyone and that he has gone out of his way to help and share what he has with his friends and classmates.

Little E thought about this and then said that we should *not* invite the little boy who made that hurtful comment to him to his birthday party. I could understand how he felt, but also knew that if we chose not to invite this boy, then we would be acting from the same mean-spirited place — making him also feel alienated and unwelcome.

I am a firm believer that you project in great part what you observe and learn at home. Therefore, I told Little E that we should still invite that boy — that two wrongs don't make a right, and to treat him the same way would be wrong. Little E agreed and invited him to his birthday party. I did, however, mention this incident to his teacher and she was just as upset as I was that this behavior was going on in her class. So she quickly added a lesson about acceptance to her curriculum.

Two years later, Little E was running for class president. His platform message was *"A single child cannot do much but a group of children can move mountains."* He ended his speech with, "I am only one person but everyone can come together to create a louder voice that can do good." After reading his speech aloud, both his teacher and the assistant principal had tears in their eyes. Little E won by a landslide!

I also have an older daughter and she was my first foray into motherhood. Both my children are good kids. They know that we will talk about whatever is happening in the news. They know we don't live in a world that only allows for "mom's rules". There is also room to discuss and negotiate some things. I have found that communicating openly with my children has developed trust between us and has helped them to understand that some people have a different point of view from theirs and that is okay.

Ultimately, as their mother, I consider myself their protector, their voice of reason, and their cheerleader. However, will I ever be a good enough mother for them? I don't have the answer to that. All I know is that each new day brings new experiences that allow us to assess the ever-changing definitions of what is good enough for each one of us.

Theresa Pang Law
Mother of Emily and Eric

Full Disclosure

WHEN MY DAUGHTER TAMSEN and her best friend were young teens, I took them to my room, opened the drawer of my night table, and showed them several packages of condoms. I told them, "Here are the condoms. I do not know that *you* know they're here. (Here are the condoms!) If the need should ever arise, I expect them to be used. No babies. No diseases. If I should see that the drawer is getting empty, I'll replace them, no questions asked. (Here are the blessed condoms!)."

I was chatting about this with a client of mine, who asked me if it made me uncomfortable, talking about subjects like this with my daughter. I said, "Uncomfortable? Becoming a grandmother when my daughter is still a child makes me uncomfortable. Abortions. Those make me uncomfortable. Sexually transmitted diseases. Those make me extremely uncomfortable. But teaching my daughter how to protect herself and giving her the means to do so? That is the least of my discomfort."

Sometimes the most important thing we learn from our own parents is what we don't want to do with our own kids. When I was growing up, if I dared to try to talk with my mother about things that I *really* needed to talk to someone about and to get advice on, she would have had an aneurysm and locked me in my room for the rest of my life.

That's why I have made it a point of keeping the lines of communication with my daughter wide open. I have explained to her time and again, from the time she was a little thing, that she could come and talk to me about anything. And I mean anything. It doesn't matter how bad she thinks it is, I have always told her that I wasn't going to scream and yell, or lock her in her room forever. No matter what it was, she knows that we would be able to sit down and discuss it and come up with a solution.

I also told her that if someone said not to tell her mom about something because she'd get into trouble or something bad would happen, that that was especially when she should come directly to me and tell me because that person would be lying to her.

When Tamsen was little, I developed what I like to call the "Monopoly Parenting Style". For every infraction committed the first time, you get a *Get Out of Jail Free* card. When kids do something that we know to be wrong, they honestly may not know it's wrong, as they're trying new things and learning about life.

So when your child does something for the first time, tell them to hand over their (virtual) *Get Out of Jail Free* card. Then sit down with them and explain why what they've done is something we don't do, and explain what the punishment will be if they should ever do it again. That way there are no surprises. There were a few times when Tamsen did "the thing" a second time, and she fussed when she got grounded, as promised. But I told her that she knew before she did it what the punishment would be, as we had already discussed it. She couldn't really argue with that.

As open-minded as I've always been, I have to admit that there have been a couple of discussions Tamsen and I have had that were simply too much information! I did manage, however, to regain the use of my speech and we chatted it out.

Too much information is always much better than not enough. Keep those lines of communication open and flowing!

Lynn Kane
Mother of Tamsen

Chapter 8

Healing and Transformation

"There is a potential heroine in every woman."

– Jean Shinoda Bolen

Spiritual Encounters

FORTY YEARS AGO, when I was pregnant with my only child, I was told that I needed to have a C-section because my baby was breached (in position with feet facing down first). And that if I didn't have the surgery, I could risk harm to her. At the time, I didn't know much about birthing. I was naïve, unstudied, and just trusted my doctor. Above all else, I wanted my baby to be safe. I was put under with sleeping gas and don't remember much about the procedure.

But then something completely unexpected happened. I had an out-of-body experience. It would take over 20 years after the experience for me to come to learn a bit about what I had gone through.

Still sleeping, in recovery and lying in the hospital bed, I had a dream or a vision of my dad. He was my hero, my best friend, and he died unexpectedly when I was just three months pregnant. I was shattered. I was worried. I had expected him to be there for me and to help me. In this vision, I remember expressing my anger to him, asking him why he had left me so soon. He told me that I could stay with him, or I could go back and take care of the baby I had just had. He was actually the first person to tell me that my baby was a girl because we had decided to wait until the birth to find out the sex of the baby.

I remember looking down and seeing my body lying in that hospital bed. I told my dad, "Whatever God wants me to do. I'll leave it in his hands." I then felt someone touch my arm and I opened my eyes. It was a kind nurse. I was back in my body and about to meet my baby girl. And I have taken care of her to the best of my ability since that day.

My daughter's early toddler years were difficult. Her dad and I had opened up a new business that kept us working there long hours until late at night. Even weekends. So she was often left in the care of my sister-in-law and her family. They cooked for her, fed her, bathed her, potty trained her, and cared for her through the nights during a very rough winter. And then, to make matters worse, I started to go through an extremely difficult divorce with her dad. It was one of the toughest times of my life.

Then, many years later, something else completely unexpected happened. I was given a second chance. When my daughter became pregnant I learned more about pregnancy again through her experience. I learned about natural home births in water, which was how my granddaughter came into this world. I also learned more about breastfeeding since I was told during my first few weeks postpartum that my milk was "bad" and I could not continue to breastfeed my baby.

With this second chance, I now get to do many things that I could not do before. However, it is with my granddaughter. I don't have the stressors in my life now that I had back then. I have the time and thankfully, the energy to pick my granddaughter up from school, cook for her, feed her, teach her art, and spend priceless moments with her. I even taught her how to use the potty by herself for the first time!

I still think about my dad. I miss him every day, but I know that he never really left me. We're together in spirit. And even though he would have loved to have met both his granddaughter and great-granddaughter, I feel both my parents' presence with us and watching over us.

Eida Wong
Mother of Tisha and
Grandma of Mandy

Learning to Love Myself

BECOMING A MOTHER SAVED MY LIFE. I was living unhappily for a long time, lost in a deep depression that never seemed to waver. I was drowning. I felt guilty all the time, because though it had been a hard journey to get here, I was in a happy, safe, and loving relationship.

In spite of that, with each day that passed I seemed to be stuck in that dark place, alone and lost, and not even the love of my life could help me. Yet he stayed; understanding and holding my hand every step of the way.

Being gifted with a pregnancy was like my first gasp of air. It was life. Strength. Power. I was being given a chance to get better, to be the person that I had always dreamed I could be — to be a mother. For the first time in my life I was motivated. I had so much to live for and so much to come. I knew I needed to better myself and more than anything, for the first time in my life, I wanted to live.

I waited for something to go wrong throughout my entire pregnancy. I waited for someone to tell me it had all been a joke. But, of course, it never came. It was the voice inside my head telling me lies again, but at least I knew that, and I could stand up to it. So I did.

Before my daughter was born, I was a nervous person and riddled in anxiety; some days I couldn't leave the house, some days I couldn't even get out of bed. With the help of a fantastic mental health team, I took my first tentative steps into motherhood and I succeeded, from exclusively breastfeeding, to finally gathering enough courage to leave the house to meet other mums. I did it!

Being a mum is the biggest adventure of my life. It has meant accepting things that I'd previously been conditioned to ignore. It has meant getting help and looking forwards instead of back. I've learnt a lot of things about myself and with a constant, strong support network I have even learnt to forgive myself. To be kind. I've learnt that my depression doesn't define me and I won't ever let it control me again. I strive to be the best person I can for my daughter; for me, that's managing my mental health and always trying my best, even if my mind is telling me that my best will never be good enough.

Luckily my body had better ideas than my mind, and at 37+2 weeks pregnant, Evelynn was born at home as planned, surrounded by her loving family as I sipped tea and relaxed in a birthing pool whilst watching Disney films. It was the most empowering and surreal experience of my life. I will never forget the way my beautiful, tiny daughter looked at me as I lifted her out the water. She was so calm and looked at me like I was her whole world; my heart swelled with love and almost two years on that feeling has never once wavered.

Amanda Colin
Mother of Evelynn

Finally Free to be Me

I WAS RAISED TO BELIEVE that when I got married, it was until "death do you part." However, when my marriage grew toxic after finding out that I couldn't have a second child, I became confused, lonely, full of anxiety and sadness. However, divorce was never an option for me.

While mimicking my own mother's traits of sacrificing her happiness and joy to help and please others, I exemplified this for my own family since this was what seemed "normal" to me.

My loving ways only made me more naïve in my marriage, and I often just made excuses for my husband when I was being mistreated. The more loving I was, the crueler his behavior felt towards me. As my marriage slowly fell apart, my heart broke, and while my mind became more confused, my self-esteem and self-worth steadily declined. But worst of all, I felt invisible and unloved.

I was miserable, confused and trapped by my own religious beliefs that divorce was not an option. I became so overwhelmed and exhausted, both emotionally and physically, that my body became weak and tired, and I was constantly sick. I struggled with constant internal mixed emotions, until a pivotal moment marked a change in my thoughts and I made a decision to leave my 12-year marriage.

I vowed that I wanted my daughter to have a different example of how a husband treats his wife, and how a father treats his daughter.

At that moment, I chose to break an unconscious cycle of mistreatment and empower us both for a better future. I endured so many obstacles and struggles as a result of my divorce, yet I can peacefully and confidently say that I made the right choice not to stay in a toxic marriage just "to keep the family together" (which was the advice that I had heard so often).

By making this decision to live in peace and harmony, I am teaching my teenage daughter how to care and love herself, despite past mistakes, decisions, and judgments; to show her that none of us are perfect, but that what is most important is self-love and valuing oneself.

Through my work as a healer and my self-care practices like yoga, prayer and meditation, I am able to be a better role model for my daughter. I hope to show her the strength, peace, and self-awareness that I cultivate, and I try to help her to develop them within herself as well.

I truly believe that our bodies have an innate inner wisdom that we need to listen to more often. I strive to help my daughter learn and connect with the wisdom of her body, her "gut instinct", and to *listen* to the way her body responds to her different emotions.

I believe that we are all worthy of respect and love in any relationship, but that it starts with loving and respecting ourselves first.

Tracy Lin
Mother of Emma

www.tracylinpt.com

Coming Home to the Heart

THERE IS, FINALLY, LOVE IN MY HOME. But that was not how my life started. My own mother never showed me love. She abandoned me as a child and went to live with another man.

Thankfully, I was raised by my grandmother. However, she wasn't able to teach me the life lessons that I needed to know. So at the age of 14, I met a guy, went to live with him, and soon found myself pregnant with my first son.

Unfortunately, the father of my baby was an alcoholic and after I gave birth, he started to become violent towards me. He spent his money on alcohol while my baby and I had nothing. When my baby was three months old, I went looking for work cleaning homes as I never finished school and was unable to read and write. With the small amount of money that I made, I could barely buy food for my son and I. I spent my nights alone, crying and holding my baby, while my partner was out drinking.

And I suffered that fate until one dreadful night when he came back drunk and attacked me. We struggled and when he eventually passed out, I took my son and left him forever. We were safe at last.

I later went to live with my biological mother because it was the only place I could go to and still work. It was a difficult time as she felt no love for me and even less for my child. She often would not even bother to feed him, and when I would return from work, she had not given him anything to eat for the entire day. This continued on for the next three years until I met a new man. Together, we created a home and I had my second son with him.

In the beginning, he accepted my firstborn son and we all lived happily together. But then things changed and he started to drink as well and became unfaithful. I put up with him for many years as I felt I had to for my two sons — to give them food and shelter while I worked.

My youngest son was very rebellious in his adolescence and often times I didn't know if he would even come home alive. But I did not let this get the best of me. I poured love into him, sought therapy and help for him, and in the end, it worked. He is now a grown adult, married to a lovely woman, and they have a beautiful son and daughter. My oldest son graduated with a college degree and is a responsible working professional. Both my sons are loving and kind and I could not be more proud of them.

But my heart did not heal and open fully until I became a grandmother.

At first, when I received the news, I was not happy. I was worried and didn't want my son and his wife to endure the same suffering as I had experienced. I knew that family discord would not have been good for any of us. Even after my grandson was born, I was still rather upset.

It wasn't until he was six months old that I began to feel so much love for him. A year later, I again received news. This time I was going to have a granddaughter. And again, I was upset and found myself back in the worry of "What if it doesn't work out for them?"

But when my granddaughter was three months old, again, my heart began to open more and since that day, my life has changed. It's as if I had birthed these two babies myself. I think about them all day long.

So my story as a mother and now grandmother has come into a full circle. The cycle of pain has ended with me and I have an overflowing amount of love for my sons, my daughter-in-law, and my grandchildren.

Catalina Cabrera
Mother of Mack and Luis,
Grandmother of Diegito and
Milena

Mother, Heal Thyself

I KNEW BECOMING A MOM would bring about some changes, but becoming a mom of twins (a boy and a girl) after I already had one young child, really took me deeper into my own wounds and made me reflect on the way I truly wanted to mother my children.

Motherhood opened the doors for me to heal my own "mother wound". Growing up, I watched how my mother never had time for herself. She never asked for help and as a result, I saw how she became bitter, angry, and resentful. I saw myself on the same path. I felt doomed and isolated, alone and with little joy, although on the outside, others would have thought I had every reason to be happy.

I soon realized that I needed to find a way to get support beyond my husband. What worked for me through this transition was to reach out to local groups and programs before my twins were even born. I did my research and asked my midwife for supporting resources.

I enrolled myself in a program for new moms. Even though I was not a new mom, I was certainly new to having multiples; a whole other ball game. A caseworker, also a woman, came to my home on a weekly basis to ensure we were all growing and adjusting well. I am endlessly grateful for this community and support.

Once I became more comfortable with my new mommy role and my children were in daycare, I attended weekly therapy sessions to assist me in finding my way back to myself while I continued to adjust to the changes of my growing family.

Out of my own experience with despair and loneliness, I started to become an advocate for the self-care of other women and moms. I've since then dedicated myself to monthly sisterhood and motherhood healing circles in my local community.

I believe that it is *essential* that women and aspiring moms ask for support and help. We are not meant to navigate these transitions on our own. The saying, "It takes a village to raise a child" is very much true and unfortunately something that has become less and less available to parents. Nonetheless, it does take a village — whether it's daycare, mommy helpers, sitters or community programs. Find the support that works for you!

Three Tips For a Mommy of Multiples:

1. Do not wake them up at the same time for feedings. I found it to be much easier to feed my babies a half hour apart. I didn't intend on feeding them this way, but that was their own natural schedule so I honored that and it happened to work in my favor too.
2. Try to be consistent with nap time. Two or more babies awake is far more tiring than just one. This also helps you get a mommy-break while they're napping. Sometimes with one baby, we feel we can negotiate nap time, but I've found having multiples is different.
3. Ask for help. Allow and receive it. You do yourself and your family a great service by allowing yourself to "receive".

Ibetliza Frias
Mother of one, plus twins, and stepmom to one

www.divine-motherhood.com

Leadership in Motherhood

MOMENTS BEFORE TAKING MY SECOND CHILD HOME from the hospital in 2013, I had a panic attack. Doctors rushed in, oxygen was given. My left eye swelled shut and I was quarantined. What was going on? Nevermind my body was completely rejecting me, how was I going to survive with another baby? I had two stepkids, a creative business, how was I going to do it all?

This was me: mom, stepmom, wife, female entrepreneur, mid-30-something creative, the list goes on. The pressure of being perfect at all of these roles was overwhelming. I was exhausted. I had lost my inner being, my authentic sense of self. My body literally stopped me in my tracks. It took a team of doctors, two life coaches, and a Buddhist monk to finally surrender my perfectionism.

Here's a sliver of my story: In 2009 I married a man with two boys who were four and seven years old. I also started my first business, Step Brightly Creative. I was a designer, creating websites for stationery businesses, designing books for powerful women leaders, launching businesses into the world with perfect attention to detail. I was paid, in essence, to deliver perfection, and I was really good at it! My business was thriving.

I took that perfectionism right into my marriage and new role as a stepmom. And failed royally. I was an automatic mother with zero experience being a wife or mom. On the outside, you'd never know. I kept up the facade of perfection on Instagram, in my business, never letting on the internal overwhelm that came with being a stepmom or a new wife. Sound exhausting? It was.

Years later, my body said: No. Stop. After deep reflection, I realized the panic attack, and what turned out to be stress-induced shingles (at age 37!), were God's gift to kill my perfectionism and surrender. Surrender to what? Good Q. Surrender and become the leader of my life. Shedding the cultural roles society places on working mothers, and instead, declaring what motherhood, business and career, and most importantly, self-love means to me.

For me this came in a few ways: I hired a life coach to help me define what "having it all" meant to me. I surrendered my perfect mom role, it wasn't real to begin with. I defined what love and delight looked like for me and searched for it in everyday moments. I didn't have to do anything, I could just smile and be in the presence of love with my family.

I sought peace. I made it a priority to meditate weekly with a Buddhist monk. I knew meditating on my own would never work (my ego is too shifty) so I scheduled a meditation appointment like I would any client meeting. I surrendered and asked for support. I hired full-time daycare, a housecleaner, I ordered groceries through a delivery service and hired a designer and developer to help with my business. I gave up trying to be organic about it all, and I asked my husband to divide up the chores in a healthy and equal way.

I focused on self-love instead of performance. Who was I trying to be perfect for anyways? As the leader of my life, I am my biggest asset. I surrendered to taking care of me first, as self-care is not selfish, it's a priority.

"Having it all" looks different for every mother. Know that this is your life, you only have one, how you choose to fill your days, your mindset, and who you are being about it "all" is your choice. Be you, be the leader of your life.

Lisa Guillot
Mother of Catalina and Julien,
Stepmother to Sam and Ben

www.bebrightlisa.com

A Single Mom's Spirit

GROWING UP AS THE CHILD of a single mother, I remember realizing at an early age how difficult it was being alone, and knowing when I was a mother that I wanted to find a way to support my children while being able to be present for them.

Fast forward to my adulthood, I found myself as a single mother and still wanting to hold true to my ideals and to find a way to carry out what I had promised myself years earlier. Although parenting alone is no walk in the park, I wouldn't change having my daughter for the world.

This experience has taught me so many things. It has helped me realize many things about myself, and it has shown me how much I really can accomplish. I have been told that I am resourceful. I have discovered that I am strong and can always survive no matter what, and now I am learning that I can follow my dreams along with everything else that I do, which I feel is also a wonderful gift to give my daughter. I want her to see her mother go after what she wants and pursue a career that makes her soul sing.

I have always believed that "if there is a will, there is a way" and that has helped me to never give up when times have been hard. It feels far from fair or easy, being that many men make more money than women, even though it's the women who tend to be the ones who end up carrying the majority of the responsibility for their children if a relationship doesn't work out. But I had faith that I could find a way.

I was unwilling to compromise staying home with my daughter when she was little which was very important to me, but I needed to support us. So I found a family that needed a nanny and would allow me to bring her, which gave me the opportunity to raise them together.

This eventually led me to start a home daycare, which ended up being some of the most wonderful years and memories of my daughter's childhood. I have since moved into the field of education and I have always loved working with children, but I also wanted to have a career that could evolve alongside my daughter so my career could grow as we did.

Now that my daughter is a bit older and more independent, I will finally be going back to school to complete my degree. I have decided to go for something less "practical", and more of my true passion.

My mother raised me to not put high importance on material things, but rather what I learned and appreciated instead was how important spending time with your children truly is. What's most important to me is the relationship and bond I have with my daughter, is that she feels that I am present in her life. We have a great connection — she confides in me, seeks out my advice, and we laugh and joke with each other until our stomachs ache.

Being a single mom and having less has made me feel in certain ways that I actually have so much more. It has truly been a blessing in disguise.

Nadia Estrella
Mother of Katia

Mama Phoenix Rises

I CONCEIVED MY FIRST CHILD in my last year of college. Young, completely unprepared and scared, but nonetheless guided. I was barely an adult myself and broke. Not just broke, but in debt for having put myself through college. I was the first person in my family to choose to go to college and I was afraid of throwing away opportunities if I decided to have a child. But boy, was I ever glad I chose to have my son!

You see, I too came from a young mother who didn't have the means to raise me, and I watched her suffer. Yet, something told me I could do this and do it well. Although nervous, I felt the enormity of life growing inside of me — a seed to be nurtured. And having strong role models and professors at my college, my decision was supported. I remember my professor from India with whom I practiced yoga saying to me, "I take it you are not celibate." And my songwriting Jazz professor seeing my pregnant belly and singing, "Times have changed!" I was lucky to be around strong, funny, and liberal adults who did not shame me. I sought inspiration because I had chosen education.

As a mother, you must be willing to embrace joy, respect, sorrow, and to always learn. I vowed to make motherhood a mission. My younger brother died by suicide when he was 30 years old. I needed to rewrite my family's history.

I had another beautiful, wild-spirited baby girl, but also went through a divorce and the death of my father. I followed a spiritual path to the divine to help lift and heal some of the powerful events of life. My relationship with *The Big Mother* was revealed and I was strengthened and certain that emotional intelligence, unconditional love, and spiritual guidance would be the recipe for my children to flourish.

Fast forward 18 years — my son has been accepted into four colleges, he's an athlete, and most importantly, he feels loved. My daughter is 11 and she's an artist, guitar player, and a loving soul. I have many more steps to take, one foot after the other on this journey, this road of motherhood, but I always look for the teachers.

Whatever your spiritual and educational path may be, please do nurture it. For I have fallen many times, but I feel Mother Earth's nudges that tell me to continue and to rise up.

Motherhood has now reached into my profession as I am a public school teacher and I run a school garden for children. I'm also a songwriter and a friend.

Motherhood is the most spiritual rite of passage that women are gifted. "Use the birth for all it's worth!" My story is for the mothers who need mothering. For the broken childhoods, the dreams deferred, the renegades, and warrior goddesses who may not know the depths of their loving strength.

This is to remind mothers that their love is eternal and supported. For, "She who cannot be destroyed." *The Big Mother* guides ALL mothers.

Toni Leone (Antonietta Due)
Mother of Elias and Joon

Progressing, Step by Baby-Step

43. THAT WAS THE AGE that I had my precious child. It was a beautiful surprise, but since I suffer from anxiety and depression, a fear came over me like a high school student just finding out that she was pregnant. To me, the fear was so overwhelming that I kept telling myself "I have time not to have it." I kept repeating it until I didn't want to say it anymore.

I was terrified of screwing up this kid's life, and that I would be paying for his therapy, not college. I questioned, "Am I even worthy of having this child?" I would tell myself, "I'm a screw-up. My mental illness will be his. Why did this happen to me? This is a gift I don't deserve."

After he was born, there were many times when I would get in my car and just leave or worse. As time went on, I grew more accepting of this child. I didn't know if I loved him or not, but I kept taking care of him. I didn't think these feelings were normal and still don't. I continued on like this for a while.

But then, something strange happened. When he was about six months old, he tried sitting up but couldn't. He tried and tried and finally got it. I celebrated that moment in our lives! A little bit of light was shining in my heart — my wall was coming down, brick by brick. As life continued on, it was fascinating to see him just discover things that we, as a society, take for granted.

Then one day, as I was about to change his diaper he said, "I love you, Mommy" (but in Spanish, "Teamo, Mami"). And my wall just came crumbling down, to the point where I fell to my knees and started crying. At that exact moment, I realized that I was falling in love with this creature of nature.

I'm now 45 and he is two, and every day, I fall in love with him more and more. My depression still exists. I have my good days and my bad days. I am learning that this is a process, not a destination. That life can give you what you think you can't handle, but you see what happens.

All I can ask for is to keep loving this child and to learn how to handle what comes next. Because I am not perfect. But it's about progress, not perfection.

Yolanda Peruffo
Mother of Teddy

Chapter 9

Strength

"Just like moons and like suns,
With the certainty of tides,
Just like hopes springing high,
Still I'll rise."

– Dr. Maya Angelou

The Sunshine after the Storm

OUR FIRST ATTEMPT AT GETTING PREGNANT didn't work out as hoped, so I felt beyond blessed to get pregnant again and was thrilled to start our family. However, at 31 weeks into my pregnancy, I didn't feel my normal self — a health-conscious yogini who proudly ticks every "not applicable" box at the doctor's office when asked about risk for disease.

I began to experience intense contractions and severe pain. I had to stop walking every few blocks to breathe and stretch. I went to the Emergency Room twice and was sent home. And finally, after a number of doctor visits, ultrasounds, an MRI and a biopsy, the tumor growing inside of me was discovered and confirmed to be cancerous.

Several sleepless nights propped up by every single pillow I could get my hands on led me to a quote by Susan Sontag that truly helped me navigate the stormy waters of my mind. It said, "*Everyone who is born holds dual citizenship, in the kingdom of the well and in the kingdom of the sick. Although we all prefer to use only the good passport, sooner or later each of us is obliged, at least for a spell, to identify ourselves as citizens of that other place.*"

I had to accept my situation in order for me to fight. These are my cards and I absolutely had to make it through this unexpected and major hiccup in my pregnancy. It was the only option. Our baby girl needed me. Although things seemingly went upside down, there was not a minute that went by that I did not feel the love, prayers, and positivity that surrounded me.

And so, at 34 weeks pregnant, I walked into the Operating Room and was greeted by a gentle army in preparation for my C-section. After the surgery, I was able to hold our healthy baby girl, Anjalise, for a matter of seconds before the team went in to remove my tumor, along with one ovary and then diagnose me with Stage IIB Fallopian Tube Cancer. Anjalise truly saved my life and we won our first of many battles that day.

Two weeks following my surgery, I went onto a fertility treatment to preserve my eggs, 18 rounds of chemotherapy, a second surgery to remove my one remaining ovary, my uterus, spleen and appendix! However, the smile on Anjalise's face and the unwavering support of my rock solid husband helped me to keep pushing forward with every single day.

Finally, I made it! Cancer-free. I breathe deeply and enjoy every second of being a mom as I follow in the footsteps of my own mom, who truly set the bar high. I have convinced myself that Anjalise was too young to remember my hairless, eyelash-less, eyebrow-less, alternating wig days. I often forget what those days were like myself.

My heart, however, is forever changed. Life matters, time matters, every single day matters. God blessed us with an angel. Anjalise makes motherhood a dream come true. I hope and pray that she continues to grow into her courageous, gentle, determined human self on this journey we call life.

Zaida Zamorano
Mother of Anjalise Vida

Stronger than Yesterday

I WAS GIVEN A DELICATE FLOWER to care for and protect. My first born, Brandon, is a child that came with a number of special needs. I remember being terrified as he was my first child and I had no idea how to care for him.

At first, my perception of parenting was at total odds with what real parenting is about. It's easy to think and believe it's simple when your own mother made it seem like it was growing up. The truth is, it's the most profound experience you will ever face. Your journey as a parent is unique and what may have worked for your parents will not necessarily work for you. I have made many mistakes along the way, but each day I wake up with knowledge and a new found strength.

Things that seem so common and basic to a typical person are a struggle for Brandon. It takes patience and repetition for him to learn things. There are always challenges to conquer. Sometimes I just want out. I don't want to be a mom of a special needs child. It's too difficult. Too many restrictions. Too many behavior modifications. I get overwhelmed and lost. Feelings of resentment and hopelessness consume me. That's when I know it's time to take a step back and take care of myself.

It's not that I don't love my child. I love him with every fiber of my being. Brandon has been my biggest teacher in life. But moms of special needs children are human after all. I simply wasn't ready to be this type of mom. But I believe I was chosen, and at times, I have to remind myself of that and that the Lord puts people I consider to be living angels in my path to help get me through the difficult times. It's as if to say, "You're not alone. You will never be alone." Sometimes I know it's His work when someone uplifts me or provides a random act of kindness. I am blessed. I don't do this alone. I can't imagine doing this without my village. It takes a caring one to raise a special needs child.

My second son, Adrian, is a gift to me and his brother. There's no one more patient and giving. He's had to sacrifice time and attention many times. Adrian's heart is sensitive, caring and unselfish. I'm grateful for him. He is my greatest helper. I'm conscious of his sacrifices. It's extremely important to me that I am careful with his well-being as well. I split myself between them, ensuring that they each get their own time and attention with me.

My sons give me strength, creativity, and the passion to persevere. Brandon's smile and the sound of his laugh fill me like nothing else. I wish I could enter his world for just one day, to see and feel what he does. Adrian's selflessness inspires me to be the best mom that I can be.

Lisandra Gutierrez
Mother of Brandon and Adrian

Birth Power

AS A MOTHER OF FOUR, who birthed all my babies at home, naturally, and in water, I can tell you one important thing and it is this: becoming a mother will make you stronger. Regardless of whether you birthed your baby naturally or not, you become a mother — a superhero.

For me, the experience of birthing is the most transcendental experience I've had in my life. I recommend that all women do what they can to try and have a natural birth, and not fear it, but rather embrace fear as a natural part of life. I know for some women, a natural birth may not be possible, but in my experience, nothing has prepared me more mentally and probably emotionally, for the roller coaster of motherhood than having a natural birth.

I believe moms need to be strong, brave, and vulnerable at the same time. And all of this happens while birthing. It's an incredible achievement.

As mothers, we become heroes. Heroes for our children, our family, and most of all, we become our own hero. There are things that happen during this mothering experience in life that we never planned for, that we never expected and yet, they happen. There are incredibly happy moments, as well as the heart-wrenching moments that we go through, and in the end, it's all part of the experience of being vulnerable. Ultimately, the journey of motherhood invites us to be open to all of this.

Being a mother is an experience that no one can truly prepare you for, and no matter how much you read about it, you won't be able to know exactly what to expect. Perhaps, the best advice is to expect unexpected experiences, both physically and emotionally. Because they will happen. We just have to open our hearts and know that it's all part of this thing called being a mother.

This is not a job to be perfect at. This is a journey of self-discovery, self-growth, and true love.

Jackie Montoya
Mother of Sarah, Leah, David and Moises

www.jackiemdecor.com

Surviving and Thriving in Motherhood

I WAS SO LUCKY TO HAVE FOUND a group of mums who had babies the same age as mine. Every week I would go to support meetings on the verge of crying because mybaby wasn't eating properly or sleeping well. Only to find a chorus of "Me too's!" These mums saved my sanity and provided my safety net and I will always be indebted to them.

I wish we still lived in villages, with extended families surrounding us and neighbors becoming family. I wish we still passed on our womanly wisdom and knowledge from generation to generation. I wish childbirth had a place and was more celebrated by the wider community so that mums and children could get the support they need.

Childbirth has been so institutionalized and marginalized by healthcare companies, often traumatizing the mother and families and wreaking havoc in a situation which should be natural and celebrated. Not intervened with by drugs and charged for every piece of tissue paper used.

I want future mothers to know that our bodies are wondrous sentient beings, regulating body temperature and milk production to perfectly suit your babies. Trust yourself. Surround yourself with equally minded individuals who will support you on your journey. This will be your most celebrated and important time of your life. Do not stress. Believe others when they tell you *this too shall pass*.

Millions of women go through what you may go through. Trust the process. You are never a terrible mother. Millions of women think that too. You are a beautiful human being doing the best you can do, with the best that you have.

I wish we had a far-reaching support network of earth mothers to help each other on our journey. But our society has become so fragmented that it's hard to find support and to grow into the mother you should be — confident, relaxed, and loving. Too often we are so stressed about getting a job soon after delivery, running a hectic household, or being perfect, that we lose sight of what is important. Our kids. Being the best mother you can be.

Find your tribe. Find your support. I hope you can find a mother figure or a community who can guide you on this wondrous journey, too.

Phillipa Yoong
Mother of Tara and Chloe

Mumma on the Move

I HAVE SUFFERED FROM DEPRESSION, anxiety, and bulimia from the age of ten. I was not parented in a way that encouraged me to become a content and stable woman, though my heart craved having my own family. For me, this meant having a man to love and children to nurture.

I had my first baby when I was 24 years old and upon learning of my pregnancy, I quit smoking, drinking, and managed to quell my eating disorder.

Since his birth, a traumatic emergency cesarean, I suffered postnatal depression. I then overcame it to become the healthiest version of me. I went on to have two healing home births, yet suffered from postnatal depression again after my third baby's arrival.

When he was about 18 months old, my stress hit an all-time high and in a particularly challenging moment, I tried to end my life. It was a wake-up call to *choose life* and attempt to cultivate some self-love and self-worth.

I have stumbled many times since that day (another 18 months afterward) but feel that my children are my biggest teachers, and my experiences only help me to grow into myself even more.

In turn, I take all the lessons I have learned and use them to also help others as an AcroVinyasa™ yoga teacher, a doula, and an exercise scientist.

Parenting is relentless, thankless, and exhausting. Yet, it is also a blessing every single day. My three kids are the best things I've ever created and I am a better woman for learning how to choose love, life, and growth.

Ariel Blyth
Mumma of River, Raine, and Reef

www.themummamovement.com

Gifts from the Moon

FROM THE TIME MY DAUGHTER LUNA was born, I have learned that being a mother is about processing old fears, even healing them.

It started with breastfeeding. It was very difficult for me at first. I didn't feel that I was capable of providing her with all that she needed.

She is now three years old and that time has passed. The hardest part for me now is dealing with the infamous colds and fevers that young children often get when they start to go to school. I love her so much that I literally panic when I see her sick.

But as my journey of motherhood continues, I continue to discover over and over again how important it is to work on shifting your mind in these challenging moments. It's vital for me to live a peaceful life, where the mind and the heart lend you a helping hand.

Being Luna's mother is the best thing that has ever happened to me. When I look at her, my eyes glow, reflecting back her own bright light. She is just as her name, Luna, which means "moon". She is wise, motherly, and beautiful. She moves through her own phases and lights up life just like a full moon in the night sky.

I love being Luna's mother and I'm grateful to have the experience of pure love and happiness with each day that I write the story of my life.

To all mothers, I say: "Be strong, for you are the chosen one by that wise soul who came to this world through you."

Querube Elena Alvarado
Mother of Luna Elena

www.lunallenadetambores.com
www.ecocreandopanama.net

Chapter 10
Trust and Surrender

"Nothing ever goes away until it teaches us
what we need to know."

–Pema Chodron

Making Peace with One

WHEN MY DAUGHTER VALENTINA was three years old, my husband and I decided to try and have another baby. But a second baby did not come. We sought out medical help and were told that there was an issue with my uterus. So we proceeded with treatment. But still, no baby came.

Finally, we decided to try IVF (In Vitro Fertilization) and were so excited to have a higher probability of getting pregnant. And after months of going through this process... it didn't work. We were deeply saddened by this. But we also knew that this too would pass and there would be something to be learned from it.

Everything that I experienced from this actually awoke a deep compassion for other couples within me — couples who want so much to have a child of their own and aren't able to. I felt empathy and understanding for them, those couples who go through one treatment after another and they still don't even have a "Valentina" in their lives, and perhaps they might never have. I thought about the orphans and how it can be so difficult to adopt that couples often times just give up.

By going through this experience, I learned how to value my daughter even more. During the months that we were in the treatment process, I was more aware of how she was growing up wonderfully right before my eyes. One day she asked me if we had gone through the same process and efforts with her as we were doing now, to have a second baby. Her awareness was truly amazing.

That's when I thought about how easy it was when we first got pregnant with her. And that brought me so much peace. I wondered if all the difficulty this time around was happening for some reason that I have still yet to understand.

I also came to realize just how strong we women are. That our bodies are incredible and able to recover. That our minds are powerful. That it's possible to intensely love a baby that you haven't even had yet and at the same time remain so grounded and realistic.

We decided to stop our process of trying to get pregnant and focus on our family exactly as it is. Because the fact is, it's perfect as it is.

As I reflect on this now, it has been a very restorative month for me. I've dedicated myself to resting, to being with my daughter, and I feel grateful that we had the opportunity to make all of this possible. I feel happy, relaxed, and complete.

Karina Alvarez Bogantes
Mother of Valentina

The Mysteries and Power of Pregnancy

To be asked what motherhood means to me is a tricky question. It means a lot of different things and to pinpoint one specific thing is impossible. I've always had a motherly instinct and from a young age, I wanted children.

I was pregnant twice before I had my daughter, Emily. In fact, the same year I suffered a "molar pregnancy" (when a fertilized, yet non-viable egg implants itself in the uterus but won't come to term). Of course, we didn't know this at the time, so to me, my baby died. A few weeks passed before I was told — what did it all mean? I didn't know. But I had to move on. It wasn't good for me to keep obsessing. It is and always will be something that has affected me deeply.

My second pregnancy was on my anniversary. A quick dash to Poundland and the public toilets for a quick pregnancy test (classy, I know!) confirmed I was right. We were happy but worried; my anxiety was through the roof. Doctors confirmed, they did a bunch of tests and booked us for an early scan. However, the happiness was short-lived. At six weeks pregnant, I started bleeding — a lot heavier than the first time and I knew: baby number two was gone.

Three months later I seemed to have conceived again, within two weeks of trying! I took a test to find a very faint positive. I saw the doctor straight away and I was indeed pregnant! Every week that passed was a relief, and by week seven when we saw an ultrasound photo of our baby, I couldn't help but cry. Everything was perfect. We were having a girl! A girl!

That is, until 36 weeks into my pregnancy. She had stopped kicking as much. I told my midwife and was sent straight to the emergency department. I was monitored every two days and a plan was made for an induction at 37+5 weeks.

The day arrived and I was all prepared, but by morning I felt rubbish. I had an infection. I was rushed to have my waters popped and by 12 p.m., I needed to push. After an initial panic of the cord being wrapped around her neck, my baby girl, Emily May Rebecca, was born at 12:14 p.m. And she was healthy!

But the birth was rushed. I came out of surgery and was told I couldn't breastfeed — I was devastated. Not having that chance to initially bond impacted our connection. All these things had a negative impact on my mental health. I didn't know how I felt half the time. I cried every day. I wondered if I would ever bond with my baby. I ended up being diagnosed with anxiety, depression, insomnia, and OCD (obsessive compulsive disorder).

She is two years old now and I'd say we are closer than ever. She is my world. Honestly, I don't know what I would do without her. So I say, if the struggles never happened, then I wouldn't be the mother I am today. I sometimes struggle with my anxiety, but my depression has eased.

I'm 20 weeks pregnant now and because of Emily, I am prepared to be a mother again, she has taught me everything I know and everything I need to improve on. One day when she is older I will thank her — she is everything I wished for. But for now, I'll let her run around in her nappy like the funny little grown-up baby she is.

Katie Silcock
*Mother of Emily May Rebecca
and Olivia Anne Janet*

Reborn with Passion and Purpose

ALL THE TESTS CAME BACK NORMAL, indicating no obvious reason to pursue fertility treatments. And yet, the mystery of it all brought up my greatest fear, that I was somehow innately *broken*.

Even before I became a mother, I lived with the burning desire to have a baby. From the time I was four years old, I can remember wanting to create my own family someday. So when the time felt right to start trying, the shock of not getting pregnant was heartbreaking. I grieved after each attempt. It brought front and center my hidden belief that something was inherently *wrong with me.*

It invited me to dive deep into a process of introspection, healing, and transformation. And it became an initiation to surrender and trust more than I had ever done before.

I know many women who have struggled to become pregnant. Each one on her own journey and not to be compared to anyone else. For me, I knew this was my path, windy and agonizing as it was. But I stayed the course and rooted myself in my heart's greatest desire — to have a baby. And then, while away from our hectic routine, our little spirit baby came to us and we got pregnant!

The journey of my pregnancy took me to all new places of challenge, strength, and connection with the life that I was literally growing inside of my body. And finally, at 42 weeks, on the heels of a super full moon, my water broke and active labor ensued immediately.

Birthing our baby girl at home, in water, was the most intense, profound, and surreal experience I've had to date. I swore that she was farther along the birth canal than what my loving doctors were reporting back to me. I had never felt so completely in my body, as well as out of my body, as I felt during those five hours. I completely surrendered to *grace*. I dug deeper than I ever had before for the strength to see this birth through and finally meet our little girl. And so we did. I held her in my arms and looked upon her face with sheer amazement and total exhaustion at the same time.

Postpartum depression, sleep deprivation, recovery, and the first two years in my new role as a mother would again bring more physical and emotional challenges than I had ever expected. I sought out therapy, healers, and support from my closest friends. And while I had a handful of moms I could talk to, to whom I am so grateful for still to this day, there was a deep sense of loneliness and isolation as I continued learning moment to moment.

I had my own mother more present with me than ever before. Her support was and will always be invaluable. But there is something so powerful about mothers "mothering" together in community — to have mama friends, who can empathize with what you're going through, by your side and in your home.

When my little girl was just seven weeks old, one of my best friends and her three children came over to visit and all climbed into bed with us both. I held my baby as they lied next to us and it was just what I needed. When they were getting ready to leave, us two mamas cried in the doorway. It was a shared understanding that we did not need to voice out loud.

As the journey continues, my daughter is both my most important student and my greatest teacher. Through her, I have honed my own mother's intuition, refining my sense of what to do for her when she gets sick or needs my attention, and we continue to learn from each other with each day.

It is my highest honor to guide and teach her as she finds her place in this world. We have always tried to talk to her with dignity and respect. Of course, there are also many, many days where exhaustion, impatience, and frustration take over. But I have always made it a priority to apologize and repair as quickly as possible. To show her that part of being human is to be imperfect, and to move through a range of feelings and actions.

For me, being a mother comes with so many demands, but I strive every day to help my daughter cultivate self-worth, to speak her truth, and to connect with her own inner guidance and intuitive abilities.

Tisha Lin
Mother of Mandy

www.tishalin.com

Chapter 11

Lessons in Parenting

"From the soul realms, your child has been on a long journey of evolution and preparation for this lifetime, most of which will be veiled from her awareness unless you help her remember her true origins."

– *Carista Luminare-Rosen, Ph.D.*

The Mama Juggle

BEING A MOTHER IS LIKE BEING A JUGGLER, but with extra balls to juggle. I've always considered myself as a well-grounded person, able to keep "all the balls in the air". But becoming a mother tripled — even quadrupled — the number of balls I had to keep in the air.

It's no longer just thinking about myself. It's adding an hour to the schedule just to brush their hair. It's running out the door in my pajamas to drop off a lunchbox or a forgotten homework. It's going across the city to take them to an appointment. It's sitting for hours waiting for their rehearsals to finish. It's waking up even earlier to make the milk in the morning and to make lunches. It's taking care of myself only after I've made sure that their things are ready to go for the next day, and then sending them to sleep, saying good night, and tucking them in.

We mothers don't have a manual. We don't have instructions. We learn on the job, step by step, every single day.

Sometimes, one of those balls that I juggle drops and falls to the floor. I slip and everything gets chaotic. Everything goes wrong. Their grades at school are not what we had hoped for. The warning calls start coming in. They appear sad, upset, and rebellious. And I feel like I am not doing anything right. That my efforts are not enough and I won't be able to raise my two girls into people that can face the twists and turns of life.

But then one day, a smile appears, a challenge is overcome, there's a big bear hug and an "I love you." My heart is full of pride and my eyes water with joy as I watch them shine in their recital.

There is tremendous happiness in knowing that in spite of all the slips and doubts, that my girls know who they are. They live with values and are maturing with each day. It makes me so happy to see that they have become independent, responsible and empathetic, and are on their way to becoming great grown women.

And just like that, all the balls are once again up in the air.

Maria Jose Leal
Mother of Valerie and Flor

Peeling Back the Bubble Wrap

SEVERAL YEARS AGO, WE WERE ON VACATION and driving a very basic rental car. My daughter, Chloe, was eight years old at the time. She said she was hot, so I told her to roll down the window. "I don't know how," she replied. The car had manual, crank-style windows, not the push-button kind, which was all she knew how to use at that moment. Frankly, I was a bit stunned that my normally curious child didn't have the creative wherewithal to try the handle on her own. Or was she hesitant to take action as a learned response to my motherly blanket of caution?

Either way, I knew something had to change. Don't worry, I didn't throw all that caution to the wind. But I watched for any opportunity for her to problem-solve within safe parameters. Like many children, she loved to chase birds in the park. And like many moms, I would follow closely behind. One day, she ran after the pigeons and I stayed put, watching her from an ever greater distance as she veered around the park. I kept my eyes on her and knew she was safe. But I was waiting for her to realize she didn't know where I was and had to find her way back to me, which she did. This was a teachable moment…for both of us.

Fast forward to her tween years. While on a tour of the U.S. Capitol, Chloe got separated from us and was instantly swallowed up by the crowd. Several panic-stricken minutes later, we were reunited after she found her way to the Information desk and asked the staff for help. I rejoiced! I had my child back and I also celebrated her budding resourcefulness.

We are fortunate to live in a very safe community, so safe that we call it a "bubble". Yet I am constantly amazed at how little freedom or life experience the young people have here, and I am concerned about how they will handle life outside of this bubble. I never thought of myself as a rebel, but in an area where helicopter parenting is rampant, I suppose I was on the fringes of free-range parenting before it was a "thing."

As I write this, Chloe is now 16 and has had her driver's license for one week. For me, this week has been a time of great reflection, as she borrows my car and drives off to see a friend or go to the library, enjoying her newfound freedom. Each time she goes out, I wonder about the challenges she might face, and how she will handle them without me there to fill in the blanks.

My daughter is getting better at being resourceful, and for that, I am grateful, because I believe problem-solving is a basic life skill. To me, it seems innate, and perhaps it is. But I worry that the tendency to shield our children from life's hiccups can smother their ability to think for themselves.

Nonetheless, I trust that because my daughter has had room to fall and fail, she is better equipped to deal with the unexpected and unfamiliar. And I believe that the energy I have put into raising an adult, rather than raising a child, has been an incalculable investment in Chloe's future.

Carla Green
Mother of Chloe

www.claritydesignworks.com

Learning as We Go

I BECAME A STEPMOM AT THE AGE OF 32 to two boys, ages seven and 11. It was a tough adjustment because I wasn't a "full-fledged" parent yet. My thoughts and ideas were not weighed equally. I was in therapy at the time and my therapist helped me work through my issues, which really had nothing to do with the boys, but rather with me learning to adjust to having an instant family.

I have a nice relationship with the boys' mother and I have a great relationship with them. Ultimately, we all became a good parenting unit. I tended to be the strictest of the three of us, especially when it came to table manners and manners in general. The boys thank me for that now. My oldest son, Zach, goes to business dinners all the time and tells me that he is surprised at how horrible some people's table manners are. That makes me smile.

When the boys were 12 and 16, I became pregnant with their sister, Olivia. Olivia has three men in her life who think she is the greatest. I think she is a fantastic girl, but I have always had to be the disciplinarian. Olivia is a pretty level-headed child and I can count on one hand the temper tantrums she has had in her life. However, it wasn't until she turned 13 that I realized that we had made some mistakes.

We didn't teach her how to "fail" or accept something less than perfect. We have been lucky because she is a self-motivated child when it comes to schoolwork and projects etc. I think we got lazy because she was always bringing home straight A's and never received a B on a report card until this year, and she cried. She received four A+'s, in Math, Science, History and Latin, an A in English and a B+ in French. If I am being honest, I was disappointed too... and that makes me part of the problem.

We have to teach our children that no one is perfect. That you will receive something below an A at some point in your life, or even at many points in your life and that's ok! People in New York City, where we are, seem to turn their children into little badges of honor for themselves. I always said I wouldn't do that, but then it happened without me even realizing it.

Last year, Olivia won four awards at school, more than any other child in her class and the parents were congratulating me. I enjoyed it. Maybe a little too much. But I said to them, "Olivia is the one who actually earned it."

The hardest part of parenting is letting our children fail or experience disappointment. But they must, or they will not be able to cope later in life when the real-life disappointments come. If your child is crying over a B+ then you have some work to do.

Parenting is hard and humbling, but worth it.

Melissa Berger
Mom of Olivia, Stepmom of Zach and Ethan

Chapter 12

Blessings and Reflections

"When I count my blessings, I count you twice."

– Anonymous

Adventures in Motherhood

I GREW UP AS AN ONLY CHILD, with no cousins or small kids around me to learn from. So when I had my first baby boy, I was so scared. I was young and totally ignorant about the important and extensive knowledge of having and raising a child.

At eight months pregnant, I had a book that told me that I could have false contractions that would resemble actual labor contractions, but not to pay much attention to them. So the night that I actually gave birth, I thought my contractions were false and I followed the breathing exercises that the book provided all night long.

But then, I finally woke my husband up and we rushed to the hospital. My water broke while walking to the car! We were lucky that it was the early morning and there wasn't traffic to get through.

My first son was born as soon as we arrived at the hospital, right in the hallway, trying to get to the labor room. My expectation was that my pregnancy would be nine months long, so the surprise of my baby being born at eight months was another factor that didn't help me to figure out what was happening!

And while there are many birth stories of babies being born just fine in cars and different places, I think it's important to have a certain level of support to be with you when that moment comes. Perhaps, it's like insurance. You probably won't use it, but you want to have it in case you do need it.

After that experience, I became skeptical and would ask the doctor before I did anything. I felt scared and nervous. So much so, that I first consulted with the pediatrician when my mother-in-law told me to add a pinch of sugar to the water bottle so my baby would be more willing to drink it. In those days, many people believed that in addition to milk, water was important for babies to drink. Nowadays, this would probably seem like such a silly, trivial question to ask. But the takeaway from this for me would be, when you're not sure, then ask, seek out help, and also follow your gut instinct!

These days, my children are now grown adults and I'm also a grandmother. I cherish my family as well as the importance of cultivating friendships and staying active. This is important even for young mothers, as they grow older and gain experience with a broader perspective.

As parents, it's important to remember that we are also individuals. Once our children are grown, as we get older, we must continue to keep learning. It will help us in finding the difficult balance of making decisions that old age brings to us. And it will keep our spirit young!

Mina Poler
Mother of Maxim, Mijael and Mairon, and Grandmother of Amanda

Love Born of the Heart

OUR ADOPTION JOURNEY STARTED a couple of years after we were diagnosed with infertility. It was an easy decision to make and we never looked back.

We first started researching locally and even went to an agency. But only one factor made us decide to go overseas. We were told that if we were chosen to be the adoptive family of a baby, the final adoption could have a waiting period even if we had the baby in our house! It was then that we decided to go to China. We researched several adoption agencies and we found the right one that was based close to us.

Finally, we started our paperwork one step at a time. Our agency was great at walking us through the mounds of paperwork, and soon we were called by the agency to meet our daughter for the first time, in a photo. As soon as we saw the photo, we said yes without hesitation. It was then that the process began. We got our passports ready, our visas, and plane tickets for our trip to China to meet our daughter in person.

A few months later, we found ourselves excitedly packing and buying all that our baby might need and more. We got her room ready, and with my mom's help, we decorated it with all the Disney characters.

In May of 2000, we travelled to China with a quick stop in Tokyo, Japan, to visit some friends who had already been on this journey a few months earlier. We arrived in Guangzhou and the next day our group would be taken by bus to the orphanage to meet our daughter for the first time. I had prepared everything for this trip. But as we entered the orphanage, I lost it. I was so nervous that I was unable to even write my name down, and so my husband took over.

Finally, the moment had come and we were called to meet her — our Kaylee. The feeling was overwhelming and from that moment on, we were a family. We had come to China with the idea that we only wanted one daughter. But after a few days in China, we realized we wanted a second child. After bringing Kaylee home and settling into a routine, we immediately knew that we had to start the process again for baby number 2.

In August of 2002, we returned to China with Kaylee. But this time, we were going to pick up Kaylee's baby sister, Lauren.

It has been 18 years since we made our first trip. Kaylee graduated from high school last May, with top honors and ranked second in her class of 357 students. We are so extremely proud of her. She is now attending the University of Colorado. Lauren is a sophomore in high school, working hard in all her classes, and is excited that she will be graduating in a couple of years. We are so excited to see what the future holds in store for them both!

Feeling blessed with our two daughters, Kaylee and Lauren, we could not imagine our family any other way.No matter what, we will forever be proud parents of these two extraordinary young women.

Laura Dolloff
Mother of Kaylee and Lauren

When Spirit and Earth Collaborate

WHEN HE WAS FOUR, my son Eric, used to like to visit his grandfather in his office that was on the first floor of the building we lived in. But before going in, Eric would go out into the garden and swing on the branch of one of the trees. Then, he would go see his grandfather and sit in his office drawing and coloring. Eric was his first grandson and filled his heart with so much joy.

And so it was on a regular day, a clear and peaceful morning, just like many that Eric headed down to see his grandfather. Then, without me even realizing it, they had gone off to the open market. His grandfather used to love to go to the market to buy fresh seafood, fruits, and vegetables that had just come in from the country farms.

On the way back to the car from the market, I'm unsure of exactly when, but his grandfather started to feel unwell. He was able to make it back to his car, get Eric in the backseat, and support himself up against the hood of the car as he fell unconscious to the ground. A crowd of people came to the scene where they saw a man had fallen on the sidewalk, and a boy in the backseat of the car, all alone and confused about what was happening.

I was in my apartment when the doorbell rang. When I answered the door, I found Eric standing outside with a couple I had never seen before. In that moment, it didn't register in my mind. I didn't connect seeing Eric with these two people. I just scolded him for leaving the office and going out the main gate alone. But then, I asked him where his grandfather was.

And that's when the couple explained to me that they were from out of town and had found Eric alone in the back of the car. They told him to get into the car with them and asked him if he knew how to get back home. So this little four-year-old boy explained to them just how to get him home safely.

I then got Eric inside and in shock from finding out that my father had just passed away, I never really thanked this couple fully for bringing my dear Eric home to me. I wholeheartedly believe that those two people were angels who came to help us that day. And maybe they even had the help of my father, who had just left his physical body. May he rest in peace.

Many years later now, I am a grandmother, and one who melts over her grandchildren, over what they do, and the things they say.

One day, after taking care of my oldest grandson when he was 3, he surprised me by saying, "Grandma, I've spent the whole day loving you." And I just melted like butter right then and there. My eyes watered and I was so moved by his spontaneous and loving words.

Motherhood is a journey full of surprises. As mothers, all we can do is the best that we can in each moment, remembering that love is always nearby, and perhaps angels watching over us.

Gloria Pérez-Molina
Mother of Eric, Eloy and
Glorivette, and Grandmother of
Nicolas and Felipe

Breakfast for Dinner

As I SAT ON MY SOFA watching home videos that we had just converted to DVDs, an overwhelming sense of sadness and grief washed over me. I smiled at the wee ones on the television, running through the grass, blowing bubbles, and making silly faces.

And then, it dawned on me that my children are leaving home soon. People say that time flies. I just never knew it was at lightning speed. It seems like yesterday that I was holding my little babes in my arms as they slept so peacefully, their sweet breath on my shoulder.

I have a lot of wishes as I look back: I wish I would have relaxed a lot more when they were younger. I wish I hadn't worried so much about a clean house or laundry or dishes in my sink. I wish I hadn't been so concerned about what others would think. I wish I would have let them get messy — really messy!

I wish we would have been more spontaneous. I wish I would have only said "yes" to volunteer opportunities that allowed me to be with my children, watching them grow. I wish I hadn't read so many books and listened to my own heart.

I wish that birthdays and Christmas and every other holiday would have been crazy fun and not so organized, like breakfast for dinner or maybe only cake with dancing and music and silly string fights.

I wish bedtime hadn't been so important, and that the extra ten minutes of snuggle time was what we focused on.

I know our family has a solid foundation. I see the joy in my children's faces and love in their hearts. And yet I ask myself often, "Am I a good mom? Have I done a good enough job?"

I think we all doubt ourselves as mothers from time to time. It's hard…and beautiful, all at the same time. I trust that I'm a good mom or God wouldn't have placed Ben and Rachael in my life. I also trust that He has equipped and will continue to equip me as I face a new day and new adventures along the way.

We're all really just learning as we go and we're all connected through this wonderful journey of motherhood.

Cherish the moments you have with your children. Find gratitude for everything, including those middle of the night feedings when you get to hold them in your arms. Laugh — a lot! Be silly. Create a safe place for your kids to fall.

Extend love in whatever you do. Extend more love. Give yourself grace and know that being a mom is a beautiful gift from God.

April Haberman
Mother of Ben and Rachael

www.Good2BGirl.com

A Letter to My Dear Darling Boy

I CAN'T BELIEVE HOW MUCH YOU'VE GROWN over these past seven years. Dad and I waited such a long time for you to come along, and when you arrived, you forever changed our lives. You came into our lives like a beautiful rainbow after some difficult storms.

From the get-go, my heart simply exploded with love for you. Love, in its purest form, untainted, and without conditions. You fill our home with so much joy, love, and laughter (and routine!).

When I see the little person you're becoming, I burst with pride. You are the most generous, thoughtful, happy, loving, and understanding child I've ever known (yes, I'm probably biased). I may have played a part in guiding and shaping you, but I know deep down that it's just you. It's in your nature.

I want you to know that when you get hurt, I hurt too. Much more so than you, especially when it's someone who was mean to you and you weren't mean back. You showed them kindness and walked away.

Kindness comes so easy to you. You put others first before yourself. When things don't go your way, you remain cheerful. Though I must say, forgiveness is your greatest strength. I've seen you do this so many times and willingly too, that it puts me to shame. There are so many values that I should be teaching you, but instead, you're showing me.

There is so much that I want for you. I want you to be surrounded not only with love and happiness, but also with struggles, disappointments, and heartaches. For only through all that, will you find your strength and true self. My only hope is that you never get tainted and jaded by how the world works and that you remain kind and forgiving through it all. It's a tall order I know, but looking at the way you are now, I have faith in you. When I was your age, I didn't even come close to being the way you are now.

When I'm sad or disappointed, you lift me up. When I'm sick, you tend to me. When I'm mad, you well, you stay out of my way. When I feel like I've failed in my actions or character, or when I'm disappointed and hurt, I only have to look at you to know that YOU are my truth — the only one that truly matters. I got something gloriously right in you.

On this day, when love is celebrated all over, I celebrate you, my darling boy. You, who has shown me what love is all about. Love that I wouldn't have known had I not become your mother. Love that is constant and holds no grudges. Like I always say, "Even when I'm angry with you, I still love you, always."

You make me happy and proud to be your mum every day.

Eve Thong
Mama of Caleb

45 and Fabulous

I have a daughter… I'm a mom again…

I have a daughter? I'm a mom again?

I HAVE A DAUGHTER! I'M A MOM AGAIN!

"Have I lost my mind?" I asked myself. Maybe. But it's the best lost mind I have ever had in my life.

At age 45 with a five-month old, I am really testing the limits of multitasking. I work six days a week and average about four hours of sleep. I go to work around 2:30 a.m. and drive to different locations. In fact, I worked all the way up to the day I delivered my baby girl. I literally punched off the clock, drove myself to the hospital, and 12 hours later, I had my sweet Jade.

Although I wish I was at least ten years younger, I have no regrets. I know that my daughter is supposed to be here, right now, with me and her crazy father.

You see, I only met her father 18 months ago. He's five years younger than me and has three boys of his own (and I have two older boys, so that makes five boys altogether)! We fell in love instantly and spoke of marriage and a child.

I said to him, "Well, look, *homie*, I'm not getting any younger so if we are going to try to have a baby, we better get this thing on and poppin.'"

We agreed. I immediately started taking folic acid and prenatal vitamins and within three weeks, I was pregnant! It was the happiest day of my life, but also so scary.

I asked myself, "At my age, am I really going to do this *all over again*? What in the world am I thinking?"

I said to myself, "Jennifer, you are a real super-duper moron. And, if it's another boy, you're a complete super-duper moron!" I was definitely having a moment. I needed to internally process all the different feelings.

My pregnancy went by fast and with a gazillion doctor's appointments because, well, I was pretty much treated like a "senior citizen". These days, they really scare you about your age and the threats of Down Syndrome (DS) and birth defects — so, I took the DNA test, and it also tells you the gender of your baby. When the nurse called from the Fetal Medicine center, she was very excited to let me know that all of the test results for DS and birth defects came back *negative*!

Then, she tried to hang up and wish me a good day, but hold up *sweet pea,* she had more good news to tell. I asked her, "And the gender?" She asked back, "Oh, do you really want to know?" To which I responded, "Only if it begins with the letter G and rhymes with Pearl." She laughed and said, "YES!"

I remember the look on Chris' face when I gave him the news minutes after I got the call. He smiled all over himself. He never thought in a million years that he would ever find the woman for him *and* have a baby girl with her.

If you could see these two now, they are like two peas in a pod — inseparable!

It has been quite a wild ride this past year. We also got engaged and just moved into a house that we purchased together. We are still settling in and I'm taking my time this time. Before, I was always so quick to rush through life and get things over with.

This time, I'm going to take the time to enjoy life and these incredible moments with my daughter. I might even bake a cookie or two! Jade is worth all of it.

Jennifer Iky Kinslow
*Mother of Malcolm, Marcus
and Jade*

Write Your Own Story

A Ten-Minute Restorative Meditation Exercise for Mothers

This is a restorative and healing practice for mothers. Should any thoughts or feelings arise that you wish to release or journal about, feel free to do so at the end of this exercise.

1. Take a comfortable seated or lying down position. Lay your hands gently in your lap or by your side. Start to slow and relax every inhale and exhale, letting yourself fully arrive into your body and calm your mind.
2. Now, imagine yourself sitting in a circle of mothers in the most beautiful, peaceful place surrounded by nature. To your left and to your right, there is what seems to be an endless stream of mothers. Each one, no better, no worse, no more, and no less than the other. All mothers held equal and united together in the spirit of motherhood.

3. Now, call upon your ancestors and the women of your lineage. Some of them, you might know, while others you may have never met in this life but nonetheless, you feel connected to them. Open yourself to receive whatever possible wisdom they might want to share with you. It may be something specific, or even just a subtle sensation of comfort and love.
4. Next, imagine a soft purple light washing over your entire body, from head to toe. Let this purple light heal and restore any part of you that wishes to receive it. Allow whatever potential aspects of pregnancy, birth, disempowerment, or pain to be soothed by this gentle energy of pure and unconditional love.
5. Now, bring your awareness to the center of your chest, to your heart space. Hold the image of your children in your mind and send them all the love in your heart.
6. If there is a need to forgive yourself, other family members, or past situations, open yourself to forgiveness and freedom from resentment now. If there is a need to be more patient and understanding with yourself or anyone else, you can also do so now.
7. To close this sacred space, tune into the powerful energy of gratitude. Think of three things that you feel most grateful for as a mother. Allow yourself to feel this appreciation in every cell of your body, spreading outwards from your heart center to the tips of your fingers and toes.
8. Now, slowly, bring your awareness back to the room where you are. Open your eyes, let your energy settle, and be gentle with yourself for the rest of the day.

Remember, this is your special space. You can come back to this connection and meditation at any time — whenever you feel disconnected, alone, or lost along your path.

To receive a free audio recording of this meditation, please go to www.tishalin.com/meditation-for-mothers.

Acknowledgements and Gratitude

To my mother, my daughter, and my husband, Mijael, who went on this journey with me, from beginning to end. Let the adventures continue…

To Rebecca Kore, for your wise counsel and loving support all along the way. To Twee Merrigan, for your divine inspiration and creative ideas up on the mountain, and for your Goddess energy before and after I became a mother.

To April Haberman, Lisa Levinson, Corinda Carford, Greg Anastas, and Gabriella Ribeiro, for your recommendations, insights, and encouragement.

To the brilliant and talented team who helped me feel less alone in producing this book — Carla Green, Deb Heyrana, Amanda Colin, Natasha Parker, Wendy Maki, Rodrigo Diaz, Es Alzuade, and Michelle Davison.

To all the mothers that witnessed me, who shared their own vulnerability in sacred space at our Khalsa Way Prenatal Teacher Training at Golden Bridge Yoga, you mean more to me than you'll ever know.

To my soul sisters who believed in this project and me, who continue to uplift and inspire me beyond what words can fully describe — Tracy Lin, Lisa Fabrega, Zaida Zamorano, Jimena Mosquera, Vanessa Codorniu, Ariana Hall, and Christianna Pangalos.

To all the mothers who wanted to participate in this book but could not for various reasons, we carry the torch for you and we are always connected in the field of motherhood.

To every courageous, loving mother who came forth to share her story in this book, to empower others, and to make this world a kinder place for us all, I have infinite gratitude for each one of you. Forever.

Last but not least, a million thanks to every single one of our campaign supporters who helped make this book come fully to life!

Contributor Index

Albrizio, Mariela .... Building Blocks of Love 39

Alonso, Emy .... Balls and Dolls 27

Alvarado, Carolina .... All is Well 17

Alvarado, Querube Elena ..... Gifts from the Moon 105

Alvarez Bogantes, Karina ..... Making Peace with One 109

Berger, Melissa .... Learning as We Go 123

Bernard, Sara .... Double the Love 57

Blyth, Ariel .... Mumma on the Move 103

Brenton, Kate .... Hearing Wisdom in the Silence 31

Cabrera, Catalina .... Coming Home to the Heart 81

Caquiero, Vanessa .... Worries and Wonder 13

Colin, Amanda .... Learning to Love Myself 77

DeCerbo, Abigail .... From Clothes to Compassion 61

Devi, Paloma .... Birthing the Mother Within 19

Dienhart, Carrie .... Unraveling the Mysteries 29

Dolloff, Laura .... Love Born of the Heart 129

Estrella, Nadia .... A Single Mom's Spirit 87

Frias, Ibetliza .... Mother, Heal Thyself 83

Green, Carla .... Peeling Back the Bubble Wrap 121

Guillot, Lisa .... Leadership in Motherhood 85

Gutierrez, Lisandra .... Stronger than Yesterday 97

Groff, Mira .... Mothering is a Rite of Passage 33

Haberman, April .... Breakfast for Dinner 133

Herrera, Sandra .... Free to Choose 23

Iky Kinslow, Jennifer .... 45 and Fabulous 137

Ismaila, Shile .... Staying True to Yourself 11

Kane, Lynn .... Full Disclosure 71

Leal, Luz .... When "Bad" Works for You 45

Leal, Maria Jose .... The Mama Juggle 119

Leone, Toni .... Mama Phoenix Rises 89

Lin, Tisha .... Reborn with Passion and Purpose 113

Lin, Tracy .... Finally Free to be Me 79

Ling Horsley, Alicia .... I am Woman 21

Martinez, Jessica .... The Power of Mama's Intuition 53

Mittal, Chhavi .... Choosing Both Worlds 37

Montoya, Jackie .... Birth Power 99

Morahan, Corinne .... A Child's Gift 47

Mosquera, Jimena .... Lessons in Spilled Sauce 49

Nativ, Jordanna .... Sacred Duty 65

Pang Law, Theresa .... Little E for President! 68

Pérez-Molina, Gloria .... When Spirit and Earth Collaborate ... 131

Peruffo, Yolanda .... Progressing, Step by Baby-Step 91

Poler, Mina .... Adventures in Motherhood 127

Silcock, Katie .... The Mysteries and Power of
Pregnancy 111

Tandy, Janine .... The Gift of Presence 63

Tayara, Youmna .... Beyond the Mommy Role 41

Thong, Eve .... A Letter to My Dear Darling Boy 135

Verdoorn, Mia .... A Tale of Two Breasts 9

Witmyer, Amy .... Trusting Your Mothering Instincts 55

Wong, Eida .... Spiritual Encounters 75

Yaghi, Kinda .... Fairy-Mama Friends 7

Yoong, Phillipa .... Surviving and Thriving in
Motherhood 101

Zamorano, Zaida .... The Sunshine after the Storm 95

Zylik, Majken Linnea .... Hiring the CHO 5

About the Creator of this Book

Tisha Lin dreamed about becoming a mother and creating a family of her own from the tender age of four. Her journey to motherhood was windy and her transition into her new role as a mother was even more challenging — struggling with postpartum depression, breastfeeding, and healing her body.

Despite the training and literature that she had prepared herself with, she still found herself exhausted, frustrated, and lost in many moments. She realized that the key lifeline on the daily rollercoaster of motherhood was the connection and presence of other peer mothers, their stories, their experience, support, and wisdom.

Years later and now living with greater freedom to both create and raise her daughter, she helps women and children as a champion for mothers!

Meet Tisha at www.tishalin.com

The intention of this book is to help and impact the lives of children and mothers beyond its readers, creating a positive ripple effect in the world. Therefore, she is donating net proceeds to nonprofit organizations that support, educate and empower the lives of mothers and families.

To stay informed about these contributions, events, and special mama gifts, please sign up to receive our love notes at www.formothersbymothers.com.

Please leave your review and comments online. We love hearing from you.

For Mothers By Mothers

Join our Movement. Empower Every Mom!

Sign-up and become part of
our global mothers community at
www.formothersbymothers.com

www.ingramcontent.com/pod-product-compliance
Lightning Source LLC
Chambersburg PA
CBHW031134090426
42738CB00008B/1078